REIKI
Usui & Tibetan

MASTER
Certification Manual

Master/Teacher Level Energy Healing

By
GAIL THACKRAY

Printed in the United States of America
Reiki, Usui & Tibetan, Master Certification Manual Master/*Teacher Level Energy Healing*, Thackray, Gail

ISBN-13:
978-0-9848440-7-4
ISBN-10:
0984844074

Project Editor, Mara Krausz
Layout and design by Teagarden Designs

Published by
Indian Springs Publishing
P.O. Box 286
La Cañada, CA 91012
www.indianspringspublishing.com

With special thanks to my Reiki Master and Teacher
Pauline Landy

*My lovely aunt to whom I not only owe my Reiki Lineage but the one
responsible for putting me on my spiritual path and encouraging me to teach.*

CONTENTS

The world needs this Reiki energy desperately and in committing to becoming a Reiki Master, you are contributing to spreading this beautiful Reiki energy.

Initiation into the Master degree in Reiki does not turn someone into an Enlightened Spiritual Master, but rather to a Master of their own self and their own life's path. It is a commitment to one's self to use and spread the knowledge of Reiki and an agreement to continue to strive for one's own perfection and mastery.

CHAPTER 1

INTRODUCTION

In Japanese the Master level is called "Shinpiden" which means "Mystery Teachings." However, this is not a static height to reach nor a goal to accomplish. The sheer nature of Reiki is that it is an ever-changing, ever-evolving path.

Making the decision to become a Reiki Master is a wonderful path to choose, but you must also realize that you are making a commitment to yourself and to Spirit to integrate the Reiki energy deeply into your life. You are also making a commitment to spread the knowledge and energy of Reiki to others.

Becoming a Reiki Master enables you to pass attunements and to teach Reiki. Not all of you who become Masters will be interested in teaching. For some of you, your interest may be your own self-development, a desire to study, to integrate this energy within yourself, and to develop your spirituality. Some may have a desire to become a stronger Reiki channel and to develop their ability to give Reiki at the highest degree. However, even if you do not choose to teach Reiki, through your use of it you will still be contributing to the spread of this beautiful energy.

In committing to become a Reiki Master you are reaching the highest level of training within the Usui and Tibetan systems. However, this only encompasses the formal training. As a Master you must continue to develop your Reiki energy through practice, reading, and research, but more importantly, through time immersed in meditation and listening to your inner guidance.

In Japanese the Master Level is called "Shinpiden" which means "Mystery Teachings." However, this is not a static height to reach nor a goal to accomplish. The sheer nature of Reiki is that it is an ever-changing, ever-evolving path. It is a journey along which you continue to grow and learn, forming a deeper connection with Spirit and developing a stronger inner guidance. You will find that healings become stronger and deeper, and your sense of peace comes from within as you live life more in the flow.

Strive to Live Your Own Life Ideals

It is expected of a Reiki Master that you live your life with deeper compassion and integrity and that you strive for perfection in your own self-mastery. The following are some of the principles to contemplate in your practice as a Reiki Master and in your own life's journey.

- Take responsibility for your own life's challenges, knowing that you have drawn them to you for your soul development.

- Understanding that every difficult relationship in your life is a reflection of your energy and karma and a learning lesson for you.

- Guide others through patience and understanding without forcing your own ideals or beliefs on them. Allow their progression in spirituality without judgment.

- Listen to your own inner guidance, spiritual direction, and intuition over and above what you are "taught" to believe.

- Have an understanding and even appreciation for the difficulties in your life, knowing that they are learning experiences. Give thanks that you have guidance to help resolve them.

- Release expectations and be open to receive in ways that you do not expect.

- Know that the Universe is an endless supply and that there is no lack except for that which we bring upon ourselves out of lack of trust. Know that there is plenty for everyone and therefore there is no need for jealousy or greed.

- Be honest in your dealings with others, knowing that the only person who judges you is yourself.
- Take care of Mother Earth, all creatures, and the environment. Make a deeper commitment to give back to the world and to leave a smaller footprint.
- Live in the now, not dwelling on the past nor looking to the future. Be present in each moment.
- Learn to open your heart, to both give and receive love. Listen and communicate through your heart.
- Trust completely in Divine Source, God, or a higher power. Trust that you will be given all that you need.

The History of the Reiki Master

Historically becoming a Reiki Master has always been a great honor, one that originally was reserved for only a select few. In Chujiro Hayashi's Reiki school in Japan to become a Reiki Master you needed to dedicate years of your life. Students often trained for many years studying and practicing before they would be considered for training as a Reiki Master.

When Mrs. Takata first brought Reiki to the West she wanted to keep the sacredness of the process. It was difficult to express such dedication to Westerners, so Mrs. Takata set a high price of $10,000 to receive the Reiki Master attunement and training. Only the most serious and dedicated would consider becoming a Reiki Master. However, this also priced it out of affordability for most Reiki students. After Mrs. Takata's passing her cousin Iris Ishikuro, whom she had initiated as a Reiki Master, decided to go with her own inner guidance and reduced the price to enable many more people to become Reiki Masters. This change enabled Reiki to spread more rapidly. Now you can find hundreds of thousands of Reiki Masters all over the world. Most who have a desire to continue to the Master level are able to do so affordably.

For many years Reiki had been taught with a great degree of reverence and secrecy. The symbols were not to be shown to or shared with anyone who was not a student of Reiki. Now Reiki has become widely accessible and you can see the sacred symbols in books and on the Internet. However, it is important that you honor this work and keep this Master training sacred. Do not share this training or the symbols with those who are not initiated into Reiki.

> In becoming a Reiki Master you are now part of a Reiki lineage.

Reiki Lineage

In becoming a Reiki Master you are now part of a Reiki lineage. Similar to a family tree, your Reiki lineage can then be traced back through each Reiki Master to Dr. Usui himself. Your position in your lineage is directly after the Reiki Master who attuned you. You can see my lineage at the back of this manual.

The teachings in this manual come from the practices of Dr. Usui and the Usui lineage. I have also included teachings from the Tibetan Reiki lineage. Other tools and teachings have been passed down and if I felt they resonated with me, I have included them as well.

CHAPTER 2
LEVELS OF REIKI

When you teach Reiki to your own students it is encouraged that you take them through the customary, formal levels of Reiki. Although your style may vary slightly, it is important that these customary concepts at each level be taught.

As your students progress, their degree of self-empowerment in their own life and their healing process increases. Their level of commitment increases as well. This is a commitment on the part of each individual to change at a fundamental level. As a Reiki Master you can coach and guide your students, but the student's own self-mastery and self-reflection processes are very much a part of this. Reiki development is a different journey for each person. Be advised that not all of your students will be ready to learn and move on at the same time.

> Your role as a teacher is to encourage your students and help them to look to their inner guidance, but also to support them in their choices.

The decision to learn Reiki and develop through the levels is a personal one. Both you and your students will experience times of wonderful highs and great connection but also times of doubt or facing your own inner weaknesses.

Some Reiki Masters set waiting periods before their students can advance to each subsequent level of Reiki. This could be a few weeks or more between the first levels and sometimes even years before the Master attunement. I do not believe that there should be set waiting periods and I let each student decide for themselves when they are ready to move on to the next level. I believe that you should not be the judge of whether or not your student is ready. If and when to move on to the next level should be entirely their decision. When they are ready, Spirit will guide them. Your role as a teacher is to encourage your students and help them to look to their inner guidance but also to support them in their choices.

At Reiki Level I you received an attunement and learned how to use the Reiki energy for hands-on sessions, both to heal yourself and others. It opened up a channel in your body for the Reiki to flow. When you attune a student to Level I, you are placing all the symbols in their chakras but only activating the Power symbol in their palms. This enables your student to direct Reiki energy but only hands-on when the receiver is present. Sending distance Reiki is not possible at this level.

At Reiki Level II you received another attunement that gave you the capability to perform Reiki at a distance as well as into the future and the past. You also learned to use your intuition more, be guided by your Reiki Masters in spirit, and to feel direction from Divine Source. Three of the sacred symbols were given and you were shown how to use them in your Reiki sessions. Level II is said to be about three times stronger in power and energy than Level I. When you attune a student to Level II, you are again placing all the symbols in their chakras, but now you are also activating both the Mental/Emotional symbol and the Distance symbol in their palms. The Distance symbol enables a practitioner to send Reiki energy from a distance as well as into the future and the past. The Mental/Emotional symbol is used to give a mental/emotional healing treatment.

At Advanced Reiki Training (ART)/Level III you received the most advanced Reiki training and tools. At this level you received the Usui Master symbol and an attunement to this energy. This symbol was activated in you and you can now use it in your sessions. You were also given additional tools in Reiki and beyond that you can use while following your Reiki guides (with whom you are now more in tune) in giving your Reiki sessions.

In traditional Usui teachings the final attunement is given at this level. The Master course does not include receiving an attunement. As a Reiki Master you may choose to teach ART/Level III and the Masters as two separate courses or you may choose to combine them. Either way, your student should receive a separate certificate for the work completed at ART/Level III.

At the Master Level you receive the Tibetan Master symbol and the breath training that will give you the ability to pass attunements to others. This ability will enable you to teach Reiki. You will also be able to give self-attunements, psychic attunements, and healing attunements. It is important to be clear that initiation into the Master degree in Reiki does not mean that a person is suddenly enlightened, but rather they are committing to become a Master of their own being and to continue to learn.

During the attunement to the Master level you receive the Tibetan Master symbol. This is arguably the strongest Reiki symbol. Although you are now able to teach Reiki to others, you may want to take time to explore and develop your Reiki further before teaching, especially before teaching the Master course. You are now on your final Reiki journey. The rest is between you and your guides.

CHAPTER 3
REIKI MASTER OVERVIEW AND THE USUI MASTER SYMBOL

The Master attunement will open your chakras fully for you to become a clearer channel of Reiki energy. Your eighth chakra that started to appear as a golden ball above your Crown Chakra after your first Reiki attunement will now be more developed and perhaps it has even spread into an umbrella or golden halo. Your spiritual vibration will be higher and you will be able to connect to Spirit more easily. This may manifest in many areas of your life.

As you integrate this connection more seamlessly, you will notice your deeper spiritual bond brings positive change where life flows more easily. Your ability to manifest strengthens and you may notice that things come more quickly and easily as you are more directly connected to Source. The Master attunement is just the initiation. The real development comes over time with your expansion to the spirit world. You will continue learning along your journey but your Master training will set you on the path.

As you integrate the energies of your Master attunement more seamlessly, you will notice your deeper spiritual bond brings positive change where life flows more easily.

In your Master training you will:

- Raise and intensify your Reiki channel
- Learn the Hui Yin point
- Learn the Tibetan Violet Breath
- Pass Usui attunements, all levels (full and condensed)
- Pass Tibetan attunements, all levels
- Pass self-attunements
- Receive and pass healing attunements
- Receive and pass psychic attunements
- Pass distant attunements
- Learn to pass attunements to animals
- Receive clairvoyant messages
- Learn how to teach Reiki

THE USUI MASTER SYMBOL

Mantra: **DAI KO MYO**

Pronounced: **Die Koh Me Oh**

Color: **Violet or gold light**

I teach the Usui Master symbol at Level III and therefore cover it in greater detail in my ART/Level III manual. The following is a brief summary followed by two versions of the symbol. Use whichever version personally resonates more.

The Usui Master symbol is used to empower the practitioner to a higher level. It is also used during the passing of attunements. This symbol connects to Divine Source or the God spark within us and brings that Divine Source Energy into any space where we direct the symbol.

USUI MASTER SYMBOL
Dai Ko Myo

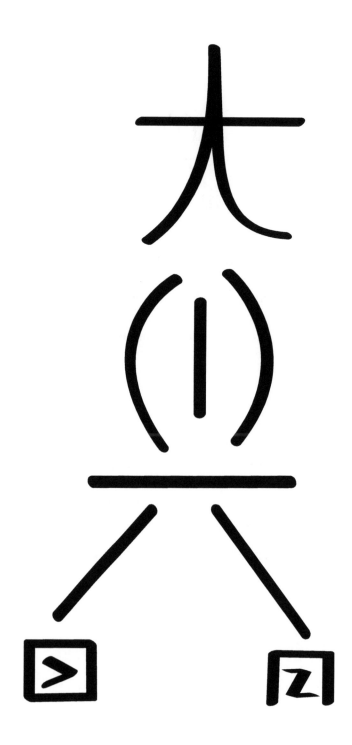

USUI MASTER SYMBOL
Dai Ko Myo

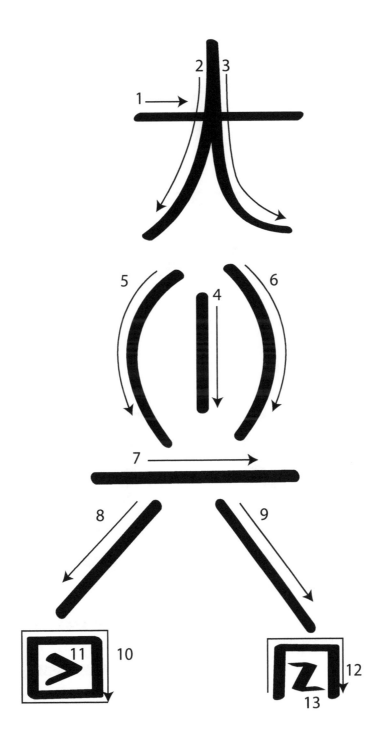

THE USUI MASTER SYMBOL
(ALTERNATIVE VERSION)
Dai Ko Myo

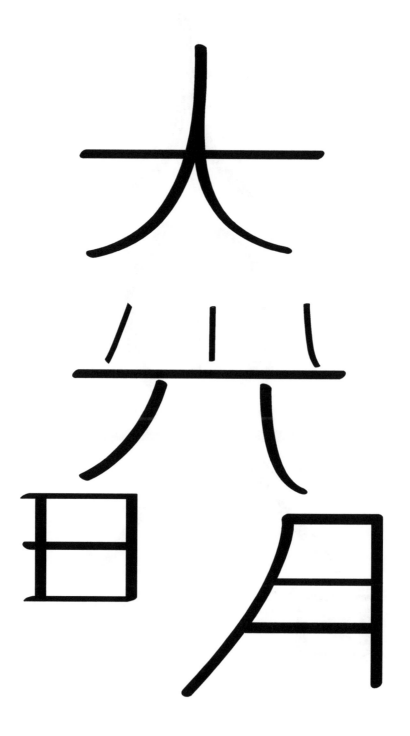

THE USUI MASTER SYMBOL
(ALTERNATIVE VERSION)
Dai Ko Myo

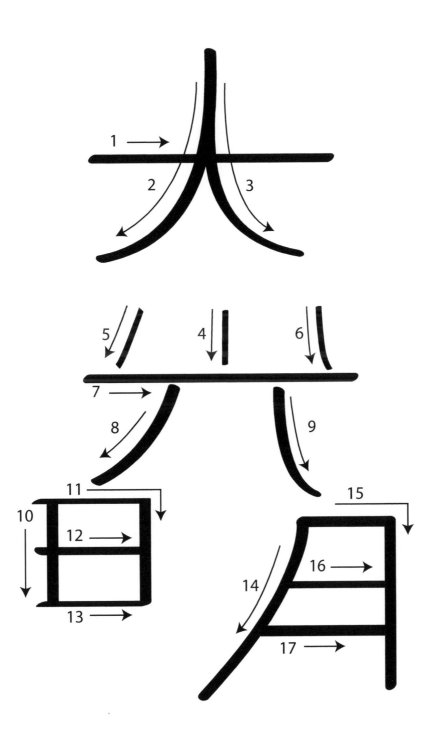

CHAPTER 4

REIKI GUIDES

When you have reached the level of Reiki Master, you are now communicating with your Reiki guides and Masters in spirit who will be the main directors of your sessions. The techniques that you have learned are now part of your bag of Reiki tools. How you use these tools will be directed by your guides in spirit. They are your partners who, if you listen carefully, will lead you during your Reiki sessions.

If you are still not seeing your guides, don't worry. They are there. Not everyone is able to sense their guides, but it does not affect the strength of the Reiki. They are working through you just as strongly. If you are having trouble sensing your guides, try using your imagination. Through your imagination the spirits are able to direct your thoughts and send messages. What you assume to be just your imagination may well turn out to be guidance from Spirit.

Some of the guides who will assist you are guides that you received through your own attunement and your lineage. As you pass attunements to others, your students may well report seeing and working with some of these same guides. Other guides will be ones that you feel a particular resonance with or connection to.

Connecting with Your Guides

It is important that you take the time to connect with your guides (and not just communicate with them during sessions with clients). I suggest that you do a meditation or visualization every day, creating your own spiritual plane where you can meet and talk with Spirit. At levels II and III you created a meditation room on the seventh plane where you felt completely at ease. This is a great place to return to each day and to invite your guides.

> It is important that you take the time to regularly connect with your guides and not just communicate with them during sessions with clients.

I like to do a short meditation just to check in with my guides every day. In particular, before doing a Reiki session or conducting a workshop, I go to my meditation room in spirit and just feel the connection with my guides. I ask to talk to my regular guides and then I ask if there are any new guides who wish to come in. I'll ask questions about my own life and, if I have clients that day, I'll ask for guidance on my client sessions as well.

I find that I connect better when I am in nature and I like to do these meditations outdoors, if possible. Taking a short walk to the stream on my ranch or through the trees usually gets me in a better frame of mind for a stronger, clearer meditation. When facing the rising sun in the morning, I find I get a particularly strong connection. Find your own special place where you feel the most connected and at ease.

I also usually do a short self-healing session before my meditation. I find that this opens my chakras and cleanses my aura, enabling me to have a stronger connection to Spirit. I call in my Reiki energy and draw the Tibetan Master symbol over my crown, envisioning Reiki energy coming down through it. I visualize each of my chakras in turn, drawing the Tibetan Master symbol over each one, visualizing them brightly rotating in the proper speed and direction for me. I may also draw the Tibetan Reiki symbol over my heart, envisioning that its energy is clearing my aura and opening me up as a direct channel.

I then begin my meditation, going up to my special meditation place on the seventh plane. I allow myself to feel and appreciate this place of love and comfort. As I check in with my spirit guides, I first ask to connect with my main personal spirit guide. Then I ask for loved ones in spirit to come through. I find that they are not instantly there, but rather I call their name in my mind and think of them. As they arrive, I feel a warm surge of love. If they are not present then I cannot visualize them nor perhaps even think of their name. Only as they come in am I able to visualize them clearly. For me it takes a couple of seconds for each to appear, but there is a clear confirmation of their connection.

Some people may visualize easily, while others receive the feeling more clearly. Some people may just feel an energy or see a light.

I may also get different sensations when particular spirits that are known to me come in. For example, with some spirits I feel fingers or electricity on my temples. With others I feel a strong warmth in my palms or a tingling in my fingers, as if they are activating the energy. When these signals are known to me, I can sometimes recognize which spirit is present.

I particularly ask to connect with the Tibetan influence, the Scribe and the Team. The Team is composed of the Tibetan monks that work with us and the Scribe is the monk who actually transcribes the symbols. (I describe this in more detail in my Level III Manual.) I especially do this if I am about to do a Reiki session. I also ask to connect with Blaji who appears as a beautiful wave of love that drops down from above. Sometimes I see her as a beautiful blonde woman with blue-green eyes and a white robe of bright light. Other times when she comes in, just her love or her light appears and not the image of a physical body.

I may ask to connect with my Native American guides and when they come, they come as three together, often accompanied by a strong smell of sweetgrass. When a powerful clearing is needed or a strong illness is to be

> If I take the time to prepare for a session by meditating, I find that the spirits come through more easily and are more actively communicating with me.

removed is when I most often ask them to be present. I will also connect with my animal guides and animal spirits, especially if I plan to do Reiki on an animal.

It is also important to allow new energies to come in, to ask and to accept the beautiful light beings that wish to work with you.

Communicating with Guides During a Session

If I take the time to prepare for a session by meditating, I find that the spirits come through more easily and are more actively communicating with me. If at any point during a session you feel you cannot connect, you can always take a moment to do so. I find it helpful to visualize going to my meditation room on the seventh plane. Even as you continue directing Reiki energy to your client, you can mentally visualize your meditation room on the seventh plane. Visualize going up there spiritually to ask for advice on the healing.

In a distance session I often find myself going to my seventh plane meditation room to ask the spirits for advice on the healing. I may also find myself traveling with my Reiki guides and my power animal to the underworld to receive an answer. I may even find myself with my Reiki guides inside the heart or a cancer cell of a client.

CHAPTER 5
BREATHING TECHNIQUES

The following breathing techniques are used for drawing in, holding, and passing the energy of the Tibetan Reiki symbols. Although the Master's intention is what is most important when passing attunements, the breath is also fundamental to the process when the Tibetan symbols are involved.

When using these breathing techniques, you will be holding the energy circuit of your body and storing the Tibetan energy in a column of light running between your head and your base. You will do this by closing the circuit at the base of your head using your tongue and at your Base Chakra using muscular contraction. The purpose of storing and holding this energy is so that you may pass it on to the student during a Tibetan attunement (or during a healing or psychic attunement) without the energy "leaking out."

The Hui Yin Point – Holding the Energy

The energy at the Base Chakra is held by contracting the Hui Yin point. In women this point is located between the vagina and the anus, and in men it is located between the scrotum and the anus.

To hold your Hui Yin point you need to contract and hold the pelvic floor muscles. This contraction holds the energy that has been brought into your body and will not allow it to drain out from your base. While holding the Hui Yin point, place the tip of your tongue on the alveolar ridge inside the mouth. This is the protuberance just behind the upper front teeth. Doing this prevents the energy from leaving out the top of your head.

During the passing of an attunement using the Tibetan symbols, the Hui Yin point needs to be held for the entire attunement. It takes practice to be able to do this. Contracting the Hui Yin point feels similar to doing Kegel exercises for women. You need to be able to contract and hold the Hui Yin point while breathing normally and moving easily around your recipient. This takes practice.

Blue Kidney Breath

Blue Kidney Breaths are used to bring the Raku energy into the body.

- When you breathe deeply and correctly, your abdomen (rather than your chest) should fill up and expand outward as you inhale. (Often this feels odd as we are used to holding in our abdomen.) Concentrate on breathing long, deep breaths. Hold your hands over your abdomen and feel it expanding as you inhale and reducing as you exhale.

- Now focus on an area above your crown and visualize the Raku energy as a deep cobalt blue mist. As you inhale deeply, visualize this mist coming down through your Crown Chakra and pulling it into your kidneys. You may want to place your hands on your abdomen to feel them expanding as you inhale and visualize the blue mist expanding in your kidneys.

- As you exhale, visualize breathing out a white mist, as if your kidneys have absorbed and stored the blue energy and you are just releasing the mist.

Violet Breath

The Violet Breath is used to transfer the Tibetan Master symbol during attunements. Sometimes it is called the Dragon's Breath.

- When you breathe deeply and correctly, your abdomen should fill up and expand outward as you inhale. Concentrate on breathing long, deep breaths. Hold your hands over your abdomen and feel it expanding as you inhale and reducing as you exhale.

- Contract and hold your Hui Yin point.

- Now focus on the area above your crown and visualize a ball of white misty light.

- As you inhale deeply visualize this white misty light entering your Crown Chakra and flowing through your tongue. See it going down the front of your body, forming a channel of light to your Hui Yin point where this energy is held.

- Hold your breath for a beat and visualize this light forming a column of white light going up from the base of your spine to the middle of your head.

- Now as you continue to breath deeply, imagine the white mist inside your head turning to blue and rotating. See it starting at the top of your head and coming forward inside the front of your face and back up the inside of the back of your head. As it spins, see it turn from blue to violet. It may then spontaneously turn gold without you trying to visualize this.

> When using these breathing techniques, you will be holding the energy circuit of your body and storing the Tibetan energy in a column of light running between your head and your base.

- When you see the Tibetan Master symbol forming inside this light, then you know the energy is ready to be released. The symbol may be gold, but it doesn't have to be.

- To pass the Tibetan Master symbol you will be blowing it into your recipient, envisioning the passing of this energy. Cup your hands over the recipient's crown and blow the symbol through the hands, directing the energy with your breath.

- If you can keep holding your Hui Yin point while blowing, this is best. However, some people cannot and it is ok if you release it while blowing and then contract it again. Holding it becomes easier with practice.

CHAPTER 6

THE TIBETAN REIKI SYMBOLS

Although the Tibetan symbols are named as such, their true origin is not known. There are differing viewpoints of their history and how they came to be a part of the Reiki tradition. Some also believe these symbols to be similar to those used in shamanism. Others believe them to be from Lemurian times. Although there are differing views as to their origin, this does not detract from the power and sacredness of these symbols.

In the Tibetan Reiki system the Tibetan symbols are used in conjunction with the Usui symbols. For example, the Usui symbols are used in Tibetan Reiki attunements (all levels). This is perhaps because Tibetan Reiki is a parallel system to the Usui system and therefore, some of the symbols are the same. It is also possible that one system is an offshoot of the other or that one system incorporated the other. If so, any information about their connection is no longer available.

The Tibetan symbols can be used in hands-on and distance healing sessions, psychic surgeries, removing cords and blocks, and in most areas that the Reiki energy is used. Basically, you may add the Tibetan symbols to most any Reiki tool you are using if you feel guided to. The Tibetan symbols are also used in some systems for passing attunements at the different levels as well as in healing and psychic attunements.

It is believed that the Tibetan Master symbol, used in conjunction with the Violet Breath, creates an extremely powerful attunement. Many attunements have become a shortened version of their original when the Tibetan Master symbol is used.

Some Reiki Masters teach only the Tibetan Master symbol instead of the Usui Master symbol. They state that the Tibetan Master symbol is a more modern, powerful version of the Usui Master symbol and therefore completely replaces it.

Using the Tibetan Symbols

You are going to be using the Tibetan symbols for passing initiation attunements (Tibetan or Usui/Tibetan combination) as well as for other attunements (psychic or healing). You will also be using the Tibetan Master symbol during your regular Reiki sessions, both hands-on and at a distance. Use the Tibetan Master symbol as guided, especially placing it first before any of the other symbols.

Don't be so concerned about drawing a symbol absolutely correct or be so nervous about drawing it wrong that it distracts you from what you are doing. Remember your INTENT is what is most important. If your intention is clear, your "Scribe" will make sure the symbols are drawn correctly. You can never send the wrong drawing or signal to Spirit.

THE TIBETAN MASTER SYMBOL

Mantra	:	**DAI KO MIO**
Pronounced	:	Die-koh-me-oh
Color	:	Gold light

The Tibetan Master symbol's name and mantra is **DAI KO MIO**. Although it is spelled differently from the Usui Master symbol (Dai Ko Myo), the pronunciation is identical. Some believe the spelling indicates a different energy or vibration from that of the Usui Master symbol, thus separating the two. However, others believe it is in fact the Usui Master symbol, just another more powerful or perhaps more modern version.

Interpretations

As well as being a very powerful healing symbol, the Tibetan Master symbol is also used to clear negative energies and blockages from a person or even a place. In this interpretation of the symbol the lightning flash inside the symbol is the light that dispels any negative energy, collecting it in the spiral. The spiral then spirals away this negative energy up to Divine Source for transmutation into positive energy. Some also believe the lightning flash to be the Tibetan Raku (see the following pages).

Many Reiki Masters have derived meaning from the symbol. Some say the two spiraling arms represent the golden mean spiral and the Fibonacci spiral. The golden mean, also known as the Divine proportion, can be traced back to Pythagoras (and perhaps even earlier). It is found throughout nature, even in the spiral shape of galaxies. Some believe it represents Divine Source. The Fibonacci spiral is named for Leonardo Fibonacci, an Italian mathematician best known for his study of what is now known as the Fibonacci sequence. The Fibonacci sequence is a mathematical series in which each number is the sum of the two previous.

The Fibonacci sequence is found throughout nature. It is thought to represent the meeting of nature, organic growth, and earth with the Divine realms. It is closely related to the golden mean. The ratios of the successive numbers in the sequence approximate the golden mean, converging on it as the Fibonacci sequence increases.

Variations

As with many of the Reiki symbols, you can find variations in the way the Tibetan Master symbol is drawn. I have included two versions in this manual. Using either one is fine. If you see this symbol drawn differently somewhere else and you feel an affinity with that version, go ahead and use the one that most resonates with you.

Use in Attunements

The Tibetan Master symbol is also used in the attunement process. It is first created within the Violet Breath and then passed into the student's Crown Chakra. When the symbol is passed, it clears the student's aura and opens their chakras in preparation to accept the other symbols in the attunement. In the Master attunement it is also placed into the hands, enabling the practitioner to now use the symbol in Reiki sessions.

Use in Healing

The Tibetan Master symbol is also used as a healing treatment symbol. It creates a powerful healing energy that is of a very high vibration and can penetrate deep into the organs. In this way it is more powerful than any of the Usui symbols combined. It can be used for conditions and issues that may not have been removed by using the Usui Reiki symbols. One may also use it to direct healing energy to a specific area in the body or a specific point in the energy of the aura. The Tibetan Master symbol is known to bring an instant aura cleansing, lighting up and dissolving negative energy in the outer bodies.

To use the Tibetan Master symbol for healing, draw the symbol over the palms of your hands. Then visualize where the energy is needed and draw the symbol over that area of the body. For a more powerful effect you can create the symbol in the Violet Breath and use it to pass the symbol over your client. Cup your hands around your mouth like a tube and direct the energy through them as you blow.

Some may find the energy of the Tibetan Master symbol to be more powerful than the Usui Master symbol and decide to use it as an alternative. Some may even decide that the Tibetan Master symbol is the only symbol needed in a treatment. Others may choose to use the Tibetan Master symbol before the other symbols in their sessions. You may be guided to draw this symbol over areas you feel need additional energy or concentrated healing. It may even be used to concentrate Reiki into a tiny cell in the body. Perhaps you feel guided to draw it over each of the chakras. Follow your guidance as to where and how the Tibetan Master symbol should be used.

You many also use the Tibetan Master symbol to power up your Reiki energy. To do this, draw the symbol over your crown followed by the Power symbol. Do the same over each of your palms. Then draw the Tibetan Master symbol over your Heart Chakra.

The Tibetan Master Symbol in the Reiki Moving Meditation

Do the Reiki Moving Meditation that you learned at ART/Level III and replace the Usui Master symbol with the more powerful Tibetan Master symbol. To do this, hold your hands over your Heart Chakra as if you are holding a ball of energy. Contract and hold your Hui Yin point. Create the Tibetan Master symbol within the Violet Breath and then when it is ready, blow the symbol into the palms of your hands, which are over your Heart Chakra. Hold the energy of the Tibetan Master symbol in your palms. This ball of energy will be a ball of golden light. As you continue with the Reiki Moving Meditation, continue to hold your Hui Yin point throughout.

TIBETAN MASTER SYMBOL

DAI KO MIO

TIBETAN MASTER SYMBOL

DAI KO MIO

TIBETAN MASTER SYMBOL

DAI KO MIO

Alternate Version

TIBETAN MASTER SYMBOL

DAI KO MIO

THE FIRE SERPENT SYMBOL

The Fire Serpent symbol, sometimes called the Fire Dragon, is thought to be a Tibetan symbol. However, the actual origin is unknown. The mantra is simply "Fire Serpent" and it is stated three times.

The Fire Serpent symbol represents the Kundalini, the life force. The seven loops of the symbol correspond to the seven major chakras. The spiral at the bottom represents the Base Chakra, which is the point of origin of the Kundalini energy. Drawing the Fire Serpent symbol over your client balances the chakras. It is used in healing as well as in attunements. Some Reiki Masters believe that this is a variation of the Raku symbol, which also appears as the lightning flash in the Tibetan Master symbol.

Drawing the Symbol

Always draw the Fire Serpent symbol from the top first, going across left to right and then going down into the spiral. It is thought to be dangerous to draw the symbol by starting with the spiral and then going up, as this would raise the energy from the base to the brain. Although drawing it in this way could be used to help a person to cross over at the end of their life by raising their spiritual vibration and the soul up and out of the body. Highly evolved Tibetan monks practice this for spiritual enlightenment. However, for most people it is not advised to draw it this way, as you do not wish the energy to leave the body unless under very controlled circumstances.

Use in Attunements

The Fire Serpent symbol may also be used to clear the aura before an attunement. During the attunement process the Fire Serpent symbol is drawn down the back of the student, saying the name "Fire Serpent" three times silently. Doing this causes all the chakras to open and join together thus allowing the student to receive the attunement in a powerful way. It may also be used to ground the Reiki energy, bringing it to Mother Earth.

Use in a Session

Before starting a Reiki session you can draw the Fire Serpent in the air over the front of the client's body with the arch over their Crown Chakra. This opens up the chakras and balances them, allowing the Reiki energies to flow more evenly throughout the client's system. The Fire Serpent symbol can also be used to enhance the Reiki flow by drawing it on your palms before placing them on the client. When doing so, clients often report feeling its energy vibrating through them in a pulsating rhythm. It is this pulsating energy that clears blocks and removes negative energy. This vibration also helps the Reiki energy to travel more deeply into the body.

TIBETAN FIRE SERPENT

TIBETAN FIRE SERPENT

THE RAKU SYMBOL

The Raku symbol is also know as the Lightning Bolt and represents "banking the fire" (sealing in the energy). It is used at the end of the attunement process to seal the process and to separate the Master's aura from the student's aura. No mantra is used when using this symbol.

The name of the symbol is pronounced **"ray-koo"** and it is drawn starting at the top, going downward. Some believe that the symbol in the center of the Tibetan Master symbol is the Raku symbol.

Clearing Spirits

In Buddhism the Raku is sometimes drawn from the bottom up to raise the spirit to help the soul of a dying person to transition. In Reiki you can use your intention to direct this symbol to remove negative energy. You can draw the symbol from the bottom up to remove negative spirit attachments, remove psychic attacks, clear spirits, and remove major illnesses. When drawing the symbol this direction, do it with caution, include some grounding preparation work, and draw the Raku first from the top down before drawing it from the bottom up. This ensures that the client remains grounded and only negative energy is removed.

Use in Attunements

Before the attunement the Raku energy is brought into and stored in the Master's body through the Blue Kidney Breaths. Take a deep breath, visualizing cobalt blue energy being drawn into the kidneys. When the Raku energy has been created in the Reiki Master, it is then available during the attunement. You do not need to blow it into the student or client. It is simply available to the Master.

The drawing of the Raku symbol is mainly used at the end of attunements to seal in the energy ("bank the fire") as well as ground the student. From the back draw the Raku starting at your student's head and going downward along the spine to the ground. During an attunement the Master's aura is connected with the student's aura. Drawing the Raku at the end simultaneously disconnects the Master's aura from the student's aura as well as "banks the fire." As you draw the Raku, you may release the Hui Yin point and release your breath.

Use in Healing

The Raku does not initiate healing energy, but instead is involved in grounding the receiver. It may also be used at the end of a healing session or at other times when additional grounding is needed. As you ask negative energy to be released, you may draw the Raku from the bottom to the top and envision this negative energy being carried up to the heavens.

RAKU

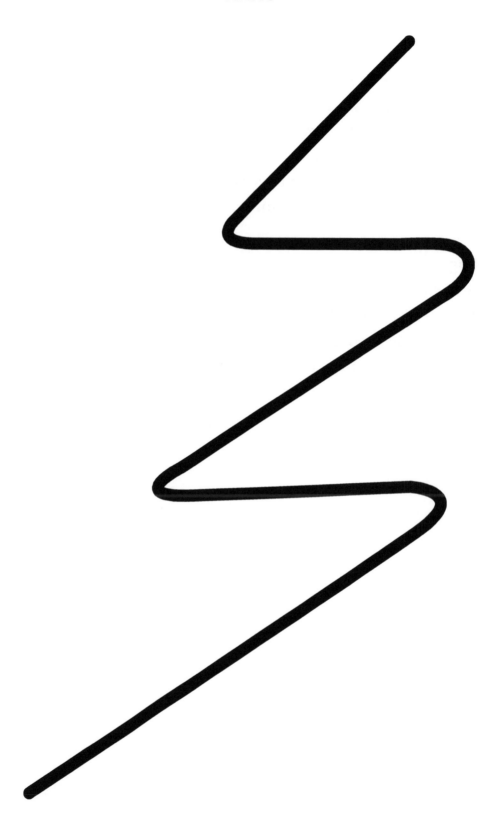

RAKU

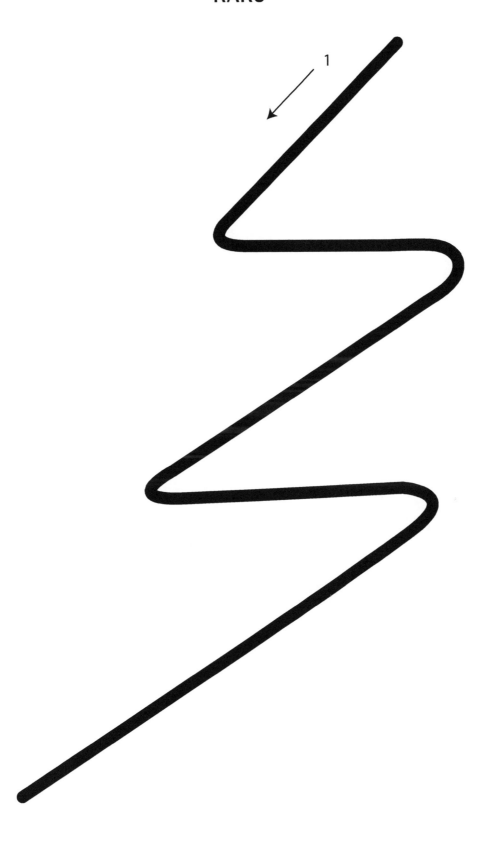

CHAPTER 7
ATTUNEMENT PREPARATION

Normally when discussing attunements, one is referring to initiatory or level attunements. This is the type of attunement first given to a student to initiate them into Reiki at Level I and then to attune them to each of the higher levels. Other attunements a Reiki Master can perform include attunements to open the psychic senses and healing attunements. Psychic and healing attunements do not initiate a person into Reiki nor do they give them any Reiki healing abilities.

An initiatory or level attunement is a sacred process or initiation whereby the Reiki Master places sacred Reiki symbols into the student's chakras to connect them to the Reiki source. This enables Reiki energy to flow through the initiate who is now a Reiki channel, able to channel Reiki energy to themselves and others.

How to Prepare the Student

Some preparation the week before will help the student to get the strongest connection out of their attunement. However, even without any preparation the student will still receive the energies and become attuned to the level intended. Their Reiki powers will also continue to enhance long after the class. The following guidelines are not something for the student to stress over, but they may help strengthen the initial experience and minimize any negative feelings afterwards. Basically they are meant to clear the body and soul and help the student to be at their peak psychic acceptance.

Immediately following any Reiki attunement there is a period of twenty-one days during which the cleansing can be acute. This can be minimized by the avoidance of red meat, tobacco, alcohol, and other chemical substances for at least three days prior to the attunement.

I send the following in an email to each student prior to their attunement, outlining suggested steps for their preparation.

1. Limit or cut out most animal protein for the 3 days prior to the attunement. Fish is fine. This is to clear any negative energies from the food consumed.

2. If you have ever fasted and enjoy this process, fasting on juice or water beforehand is good. It can be for 1-2 days or just a few hours. If you are not used to this, then just try to eat healthy.

3. Limit or stop any caffeinated drinks for 3 days.

4. Limit or don't drink alcohol for 3 days.

5. Limit or stop eating sugar or junk food for 3 days.

6. Limit or stop smoking cigarettes for 3 days.

7. Quiet negative outside distractions, news, horror movies, etc. for 3 days.

8. Try to spend some time appreciating nature each day.

9. Start as soon as possible and meditate daily, an hour if possible. If you are not able to meditate, just sit quietly and contemplate. Ask to release anger, fear, worry, and other negative feelings. Then spend some time contemplating or meditating on why you want to be attuned to Reiki (or advance to the next level) and what you wish to receive from your attunement (e.g., to increase your psychic abilities or to be able to heal yourself and others, mentally and physically).

10. If you use other rituals or methods to get your psychic powers stimulated, go ahead and use those to prepare yourself.

Again, many people do nothing beforehand so don't stress about this, but a quiet contemplating period before would be good and at least avoid a heavy party weekend!

After the Attunement

Cleansing takes place on all levels – physical, mental, emotional, and spiritual. The more the Reiki energy is allowed to flow, the more beneficial this will be. Tell your students to go easy on themselves during this time and allow the process. Drinking lots of water will help to release toxins and flush out any negative energy that has surfaced. Self-healing sessions will help them to release and cleanse more quickly. Suggest to your students to take time to meditate daily, get lots of sleep and rest, and to take walks in nature. Doing so may help them through this process.

How the Reiki Master Prepares

The Reiki Master should prepare their physical body in the same manner as the student. Try to clear your body and mind as much as possible the week before and meditate daily. Your teaching space should be prepared in the same way as you would prepare for a session, using smudging and the Reiki symbols.

CHAPTER 8
PASSING ATTUNEMENTS

The Reiki initiation or level attunements are powerful spiritual initiation rituals. This is the heart of Reiki. The attunement energy is divinely inspired and originates from Divine Source. The Reiki attunement is a transfer of energy through the Master to the student with the attunement being given by the Reiki Master's guides in spirit. This attunement aligns the student with the Universal Life Force Energy of Reiki and allows Reiki energy to channel through the body of the student.

When I first started passing attunements, I was scared that I would forget something and then what do I do? What if I did something in the wrong order? Do I go back and start again or do I repeat what I had missed? My Scribe told me not to worry; my intention is what matters and he would fix the rest. In fact, I am sure that if I just made the connection and intended for the attunement to pass, they would do the rest. Of course, I would not do that, but it is reassuring to know. The point is, if you feel like you did not do something correctly, do not worry about it. Your Reiki guides and Masters in spirit are the ones really giving the attunement. You are just the conduit. Set your intention. Say, "I am giving a Reiki Level I attunement" and try your best to perform the attunement the way that you learned to pass it. Then trust that your guides will pass the attunement instantly and in perfect ways – because they will.

> A Reiki attunement is a transfer of energy through the Master to the student with the attunement being given by the Reiki Master's guides in spirit.

You may have a student with a disability that prevents them from sitting in a chair or raising their hands above their head. An attunement can be passed to anyone, no matter the state of their physical body. It is your intention that calls in your Reiki Masters, and they are the ones that do the actual work. If you have a student that cannot receive the attunement in the way that you have been taught, ask your guides how you should improvise and what to do instead. Then follow your guidance.

Tell the Students What to Expect

I like to bring one student up in front of the class to demonstrate what will happen during the attunement. I do not perform an actual attunement, but instead I explain where I will be and what to expect by going through the approximate motions of the attunement process. I show the students that I will be touching their head, opening their hands, etc. At one point during the attunement the Master will squeeze the student's left shoulder. This is a signal to the student to raise their hands (still together) above their Crown Chakra. I practice this with my students. Although I let them know that nine times out of ten, the student is so engrossed in the sensations of what is going on that they completely forget to do this when the signal is given. Almost always I need to reach over and take the student's hands, which is perfectly fine. At this point you will have also already discussed what emotional and spiritual sensations your students may feel during and after the attunement.

Preparing Your Attunement Room

Before your students arrive you need to prepare your attunement room and, in fact, any rooms that you will be using for your Reiki workshop. You will be removing any negative energy from the rooms and positively charge them with Reiki. Express to your Reiki guides your intention to perform the attunements and in which room you intend to do so. There are several different ways to do this. The following are some of the rituals that I like to use.

1. Light a white candle, then a purple candle. As I light the white candle, I say to myself, "I light this white candle to represent Divine Source. May this white light bring positive Reiki energies into this room." As I light

the purple candle, I say to myself, "May this purple candle remove any negative energies in this room and transmute them into positive energy."

2. Smudge the room with sage. This is a Native American tradition that clears negative energies. I like to use a sage wand to smudge in the corners of the room, drawing the Power symbol. Smudge each corner, around yourself, and the chair where your student will be seated. You should have an open window for the smoke to leave along with the negative energy it is carrying away. Smudging without an open window is not as effective.

3. You may light sweetgrass or incense such as sandalwood, which brings in positive energy since the smudge has created a void. This is a Native American tradition as well.

4. You should have already done your personal Reiki protection, such as a bubble of white light protection. If this hasn't been done, do so now.

5. Call in your Reiki guides and Masters in spirit. Draw the Tibetan Master, Usui Master, and Power symbols on the palm of each of your hands. Then draw the Power symbol down the front of your body and over each of your chakras to open yourself up to the energy.

6. Stand in the center of the room and ask your Reiki guides and Masters in spirit to bless this room. See beautiful Reiki energy radiating from you out into each corner of the room and filling the entire room with beautiful Reiki energy.

7. Place all the Reiki symbols in each corner of the room. Draw them in the air and send Reiki energy into each corner. You may also use your sage wand to draw them into the corners.

8. If you have a chair set up for the attunement, repeat the blessings around it.

9. If you are using crystals in your attunement room make sure they have been cleansed of negative energies and charged with positive Reiki energy. If desired, you can charge clear quartz crystals to send positive energy throughout the attunements with the intention that they hold

and emanate Reiki energy. You could also use one type of crystal for removing negative energy from the room (such as tourmaline or smoky quartz) and then use a clear quartz crystal for positive energy.

Attunement Position

Usually the student is seated in a chair and the Reiki Master stands. The chair should have a straight back so that the Master can easily stand behind the student. You could also use a stool or bench that has no back. There should be enough space to easily move to the front of the student when required. The height of the chair should also be low enough so that the Master is able to look over the student's Crown Chakra as well as reach over the student to lift their hands, if necessary. The attunement begins with the student's hands in prayer position over their heart.

Group or Individual Attunements

I personally prefer to perform individual attunements. I take each student into a separate area where I give them their attunement. After the student has received their attunement, they may either take a snack break or do Reiki practice exercises.

Some Reiki Masters attune their students in groups where the students are lined up in rows or in a small circle, attuning one student at a time. If this is the way you plan to do it, leave enough room between the chairs to be able to easily move from the back to the front. Other Reiki Masters attune whole rows at once. In this case the Master does the "from behind" part of the attunement on each student in the row and then does the front part on each student, moving along the row until all the attunements are complete. If attunements are given in a group and some are attuned before the others are finished, all must remain in quiet meditation until the whole group is finished.

For individual attunements I allocate about 8-10 minutes per person. For six to eight students it takes about an hour to complete all the attunements. If the traditional four-stage level I attunement is used, this will take more time than the other versions.

To Begin the Attunement

1. The attunement room has already been prepared.

2. The student is instructed to sit down in a chair.

3. The student begins with their hands in prayer position over their Heart Chakra.

4. You may smudge your student if they have first agreed that this is something they would like.

5. The student is instructed to keep their eyes closed during the entire attunement process. If they are very uncomfortable with this, they can focus straight ahead at a crystal or candle flame.

6. The student is instructed to imagine Reiki energy flowing through them, coming down from their Crown Chakra, running through their body, and expanding out into their aura.

7. Start by standing behind your student with a little distance between you. Call in your Reiki guides and Masters in spirit. Draw the Usui Master, Tibetan Master, and Power symbols over your crown and the palms of each of your hands, tapping them in with the mantras. Then draw the Power symbol over the front of your body and over each chakra. Set the intention by saying, "this is to be a level I, II, or III Reiki attunement" as appropriate. Say a silent prayer asking for the help of your Reiki guides and Masters as well as your personal spirit guides.

8. For a Tibetan attunement or a Blaji attunement where the Tibetan symbols are to be used, you will be using the Blue Kidney Breath, Violet Breath, and holding the Hui Yin point. Hold the Hui Yin point while keeping your tongue pressed against the alveolar ridge for the duration of the transmission of the attunement. It is released when the attunement is finished.

9. Now connect with your student and begin the Reiki attunement.

10. REMEMBER to silently thank your Reiki guides and Masters at the end of the attunement.

PLEASE NOTE:

- During all attunements the mantras are always said silently, never out loud.

- The attunements are written as though the person giving the attunement is right-handed. For left-handed Reiki Masters, use the opposite hand position.

- When the attunements are passed into the raised hands over the Crown Chakra, the hands should be directly above the crown. For some this position may be uncomfortable. If so, do not try to force your student's hands into this position. If the students hands are more forward and not directly above the Crown Chakra, then you have the option to do an additional tap at the crown, making a total of four taps: at the hands, at the crown, at the back of the Third Eye and at the base of the brain. Alternatively, you can envision that the tap at the hands is above the crown, even if it physically is not.

- Toward the end of the attunement you are instructed to watch the symbols going into the student. This is done both when you are looking down into the crown to the Heart Chakra and also when you are looking at the triangular "door" at the back of the student's head. When you do this, visualize each symbol, one at a time, entering the student. It is best to visualize the entire symbol as a full image (and in 3-D if you can), rather than to visualize it being drawn out. You do not need to say their mantras, just visualize them going in and use your intention to direct them.

- When placing the symbols into the student's palms, you may draw and tap them into each palm individually. Alternatively, you may place your student's hands together, one on top of the other, both palms facing up. Then draw the symbols in the air over their stacked hands, envisioning the symbols going into both palms at the same time. Either method is fine; it is an individual choice. I have also heard of Reiki Masters who activate only one palm. However, I believe that it is very important to activate both palms, whether they are done individually or together.

CHAPTER 9
VARIATIONS OF ATTUNEMENTS

On your Reiki journey you are encouraged to continue your study of Reiki, to follow the guidance of your Reiki guides and Masters in spirit, and also to continue reading and researching what other Reiki Masters have developed. When I first became a Reiki Master, I was given one set of attunements, but I soon discovered through reading the teachings of other Reiki Masters that attunements are given in many different ways. There are various lineages of Reiki and in each, the method of Reiki attunement may be taught slightly different.

Just as you may see the Reiki symbols drawn in different ways, you may also see attunements given in different ways. Though the basic premise and the symbols that are placed into the student are usually the same, the order that they are given may vary. Some Reiki Masters seem to have simplified the process.

In most systems the Reiki levels are distinguished by what symbols are placed into the recipient's hands and can therefore be used by the recipient. Although all of the symbols are placed into the crown at each attunement, only some of the symbols are placed into the palms at the lower level attunements. Additional symbols are added into the palms at each subsequent level. The symbols that are placed into the palms during each level of attunement are the ones that the Reiki student can use in their sessions.

I asked my guides which system is the correct one, to which they replied, "All of them." For it is the intention of the Reiki Master that is most important and the ritual of passing the symbols is merely a ritual to connect to the intention of the Reiki Master. Still, I felt that some systems of attunement were too oversimplified and some were overly complicated.

Usui System

The Hui Yin point, Violet Breath, and Blue Kidney Breaths are not used in this system, nor are the Tibetan symbols. The first degree of Reiki is split into four attunements, given one after the other, resulting in a lengthy Level I initiatory attunement. There is only one Master attunement and this is given at ART/Level III. No attunement is given in the Master course.

Simplified Usui System

Several Reiki Masters have simplified the Usui system by performing the Level I attunement in one part. Some Masters have also further simplified other parts of the Usui attunement.

Tibetan Reiki System

In the Tibetan Reiki system the Tibetan Master symbol is used as well as all of the Usui symbols. The Tibetan Master symbol is passed in conjunction with holding the Hui Yin point and using the Violet Breath. The passing through this sacred breathing method is considered by many Reiki Masters to be so powerful that the rest of the attunement and the additional symbols are often passed in a more condensed form. Since the Tibetan attunement incorporates the Usui symbols, many Reiki Masters use the Tibetan attunement as the entire Usui/Tibetan attunement. However, the Tibetan attunement usually does not place the symbols into the Third Eye and this is the reason that some Masters give a Usui and a Tibetan attunement separately. There is only one Tibetan Master attunement and this is given at the Master level and therefore there is no Tibetan attunement at ART/Level III.

Simplified Tibetan Reiki System

Some Reiki Masters use a very simplified Tibetan Reiki attunement without using the Usui Master symbol. In this case the Tibetan Master symbol is used instead of the Usui Master symbol. The Masters who teach this method say that the Tibet Master symbol is a modern version of the Usui Master symbol, thus replacing it.

Blaji's Version – Combined Usui/Tibetan Reiki system

I meditated and asked my guides which system I should choose. I liked the power of the Tibetan system and that it also delivered the Usui symbols at the same time, but I had two issues. The first was that the symbols in the Tibetan system do not go into the Third Eye and I felt that for psychic abilities this was important. The second issue I had was at the ART and Master levels. The Usui system gives one attunement at ART/Level III and none at the Master, and the Tibetan system gives one attunement at the Master and none at ART/Level III.

I asked for permission from my guides to combine these methods and to give my students the additional symbols to the Third Eye as well as an attunement at both ART/Level III and the Master level. The version that I like to use is this combination as channeled by my guides. I call it the Blaji version after my guide Blaji. I feel that it is strong and gives my students all that is offered in both systems.

Just as you may see the Reiki symbols drawn in different ways, you may also see attunements given in different ways.

In this manual I have included the Blaji attunements, the Usui attunements (including the four-stage Level I attunement), and the Tibetan attunements. I suggest that you try the different systems and see which one feels right to you.

CHAPTER 10
SYMBOLS PASSED IN ATTUNEMENTS

The Symbols and Their Sacred Names

Tibetan Master – Dai Ko Mio

Usui Master – Dai Ko Myo

Power – Cho Ku Rei

Mental/Emotional – Sei Hei Ki

Distance – Hon Sha Za Sho Nen

Fire Serpent – Fire Serpent

SUMMARY OF THE SYMBOLS PASSED DURING ATTUNEMENTS

The following is a summary of the symbols that you will pass in each attunement. The various symbols will be placed in different areas, depending on the type of attunement and the level. The locations may include: over your student's entire back, crown, hands (while held above the crown), Third Eye, the open palms, and then the back again. The specific directions for each attunement are on the subsequent pages.

BLAJI'S VERSION – Combined Usui/Tibetan Reiki System

In Blaji's version the breath techniques are used and both the Usui and Tibetan symbols are passed. There is an attunement at each level.

Blaji – Reiki Level I

Back – Fire Serpent

Crown – Tibetan Master, Usui Master, Mental/Emotional, Distance

Hands Above Crown – Power

Third Eye – Power, Mental/Emotional, Distance

Open Palms – Power

Back – Raku

Blaji – Reiki Level II

Back – Fire Serpent

Crown – Tibetan Master, Usui Master

Hands Above Crown – Power, Mental/Emotional, Distance

Third Eye – Power, Mental/Emotional, Distance

Open Palms – Power, Mental/Emotional, Distance

Back – Raku

Blaji – Reiki Level III/ART

Back – Fire Serpent

Crown – Tibetan Master

Hands Above Crown – Usui Master, Power, Mental/Emotional, Distance

Third Eye – Usui Master, Power, Mental/Emotional, Distance

Open Palms – Usui Master, Power, Mental/Emotional, Distance

Back – Raku

Blaji – Reiki Master

Back – Fire Serpent

Hands Above Crown – Tibetan Master, Fire Serpent, Usui Master, Power, Mental/Emotional, Distance

Third Eye – Tibetan Master, Fire Serpent, Usui Master, Power, Mental/Emotional, Distance

Open Palms – Tibetan Master, Fire Serpent, Usui Master, Power, Mental/Emotional, Distance

Back – Raku

USUI SYSTEM – Long Version

In the Usui system the breath techniques are not used. Only the Usui symbols are passed and there is no attunement at the Master level. The Level I attunement is split into four attunements given consecutively.

Usui System – Reiki Level I

Crown – Usui Master, Distance, Mental/Emotional

Hands Above Crown – Power

Third Eye – Power, Mental/Emotional, Distance

Open Palms – Power

Usui System – Reiki Level II

Crown – Usui Master

Hands Above Crown – Power, Mental/Emotional, Distance

Third Eye – Power, Mental/Emotional, Distance

Open Palms – Power, Mental/Emotional, Distance

Usui System – Reiki Level III/ART

Crown – None

Hands Above Crown – Usui Master, Power, Mental/Emotional, Distance

Third Eye – Usui Master, Power, Mental/Emotional, Distance

Open Palms – Usui Master, Power, Mental/Emotional, Distance

Usui System – Reiki Master

No attunement

TIBETAN REIKI SYSTEM

In the Tibetan system the breath techniques are used to pass the Tibetan symbols. Both the Usui and Tibetan symbols are passed. The Level I attunement is split into four attunements given consecutively. There is no attunement at Reiki III/ART level.

Tibetan System – Level I

Back – Fire Serpent

Crown – Tibetan Master, Usui Master, Mental/Emotional, Distance

Hands Above Crown – Power

Open Palms – Power

Tibetan System – Level II

Back – Fire Serpent

Crown – Tibetan Master, Usui Master

Hands Above Crown – Power, Mental/Emotional, Distance

Open Palms – Power, Mental/Emotional, Distance

Tibetan System – Level III/ART

No attunement

Tibetan System – Master

Back – Fire Serpent

Crown – Tibetan Master

Hands Above Crown – Tibetan Master, Fire Serpent, Usui Master, Power, Mental/Emotional, Distance

Open Palms – Tibetan Master, Fire Serpent, Usui Master, Power, Mental/Emotional, Distance

CHAPTER 11
BLAJI'S INITIATORY ATTUNEMENTS

BLAJI'S VERSION
FIRST DEGREE ATTUNEMENT – USUI/TIBETAN

This is a combined Usui and Tibetan attunement that passes the sacred symbols from the Usui system as well as the Tibetan Master symbol and includes an attunement to the Third Eye. The Violet Breath is used and the Hui Yin point is held throughout the attunement.

The symbols that you will be passing:

Back – Fire Serpent

Crown – Tibetan Master, Usui Master, Mental/Emotional, Distance

Hands Above Crown – Power

Third Eye – Power, Mental/Emotional, Distance

Open Palms – Power

Back – Raku

From Behind

1. Standing behind your student, draw the **Fire Serpent symbol** starting at the back of your student's head going down to their Base Chakra.

2. Connect energetically by placing your hands over the top of their head, tuning in.

3. Contract and hold the Hui Yin point, keeping your tongue against the alveolar ridge (throughout the entire attunement). Take three Blue Kidney Breaths to create the Raku energy and then create the **Violet Breath**. Visualize the **Tibetan Master symbol** within the violet light and blow it into the student's head. Visualize the symbol moving from your head, through your breath, into your student's Crown Chakra, and going into the base of their brain. As you visualize this, silently say the mantra of the symbol three times and tap, once each, at the Crown Chakra, the back of the Third Eye, and at the base of the brain.

4. Draw the **Usui Master symbol over your student's head**. Visualize the symbol moving into the Crown Chakra, through the head, to the base of the brain. As you visualize this, silently say the mantra three times and tap, once each, at the Crown Chakra, the back of the Third Eye, and at the base of the brain.

5. Repeat step [4] with the **Mental/Emotional symbol over the head.**

6. Repeat step [4] with the **Distance symbol over the head.** (NOTE - YOU HAVE SKIPPED THE POWER SYMBOL)

7. Squeeze your student's left shoulder to let them know to raise their hands above their head. If they do not remember to do so, then gently pull up their hands.

8. While **holding your student's hands, draw the Power symbol** in the air above them. Visualize the symbol going into the hands, through the Crown Chakra, to the base of the brain. As you visualize this, silently say the mantra three times and tap, once each, at the fingertips over the Crown Chakra, the back of the Third Eye, and at the base of the brain.

9. Return your student's hands back down to prayer position over the heart.

From the front

1. Go to the front of your student, facing them, and **open their hands** out flat. Place your left hand underneath.

2. Draw the **Power symbol over their Third Eye**, tapping it in three times while silently saying the mantra. Visualize the symbol going into the Third Eye.

3. Repeat the step [2], drawing the **Mental/Emotional symbol over the Third Eye.**

4. Repeat the step [2], drawing the **Distance symbol over the Third Eye.**

5. Draw the **Power symbol over each of their palms**, tapping it in three times while silently saying the mantra. Visualize the symbol moving into each hand. Then using the open palm of your right hand, lightly pat three times into each of the student's open palms. (NOTE - YOU HAVE ACTIVATED ONLY THE POWER SYMBOL IN THE PALMS.)

6. **Return your student's hands** to prayer position in front of their heart. In one strong breath (if you can), blow from your student's hands down toward the Base Chakra, then up to the Third Eye, back down to the Solar Plexus, and then end back at the hands. (If you can keep your Hui Yin point contracted while blowing, that is best. If not, it is ok to release it while you blow and then contract it again.)

From behind

1. Return to the back of your student, putting your hands on their shoulders. Imagine looking down through the student's crown and into their Heart Chakra. See each of the Reiki symbols inside the chakra. Choose a positive affirmation, such as, **"You are now a powerful and aware Reiki Level I healer."** You are going to place the positive affirmation into their heart. Silently say the affirmation three times with the intention that your student's subconscious accepts it.

2. Visualize a triangular door made by placing your thumbs and fingers at the back of your student's head. Your thumbs (the base of the triangle) should be at or near the occipital ridge. See all the symbols going inside their head, one by one, and then visualize this door being closed and sealed with the Power symbol on the outside. Silently say to your guides, **"I seal this attunement with love and Divine energy."** (Or use something similar that resonates with you.) Intend that the process is complete and that your

student's direct connection to the Reiki Source and their Reiki guides is now in place.

3. Once again put your hands on your student's shoulders. Silently say to your guides, **"In this attunement we are both blessed."**

4. Draw the **Raku** Symbol down the back of your student to seal in the attunement and disconnect your aura from your student's aura. You may release the Hui Yin point as you draw the Raku.

From the front

1. Return to the front, facing your student. Place their hands on their lap, palms facing down. In the case of group attunements, this step is left until all your students have been attuned.

State a blessing aloud to let your student know the process is complete.

"You are now a powerful and aware Reiki Level I healer."

ILLUSTRATED ATTUNEMENT – BLAJI LEVEL I

1. Power Up

Protect yourself. Call in your Reiki guides and Masters. Ask the Reiki energy to flow.

2. Fire Serpent

Draw the **Fire Serpent** symbol from the top of the head to the base of the spine.

3. Connect

Place your hands over your student and feel the connection between you

4. Tibetan Master

Contract and hold the Hui Yin point, keeping your tongue against the alveolar ridge (throughout the entire attunement). Take three Blue Kidney Breaths, and then create the **Violet Breath**. Visualize the **Tibetan Master symbol** within the violet light and blow it into the student's head. Visualize the symbol moving from your head, through your breath, into your student's Crown Chakra, and going into the base of their brain.

As you visualize this, silently say the mantra of the symbol three times and tap, once each, at the Crown Chakra, the back of the Third Eye, and at the base of the brain.

5. Crown	6. Back of the Third Eye	7. Base of the Brain

Draw the **Usui Master symbol over your student's head**. Visualize the symbol moving into the Crown Chakra, through the head, to the base of the brain. As you visualize this, silently say the mantra of the symbol three times and tap, once each, at the Crown Chakra (photo 5), the back of the Third Eye (photo 6), and at the base of the brain (photo 7).

Repeat with the **Mental/Emotional and Distance symbols**.

(NOTE - YOU HAVE SKIPPED THE POWER SYMBOL)

8. Squeeze Shoulder

Squeeze their left shoulder as a signal to raise their hands to the top of their head.

9. Hands Above the Crown   10. Back of the Third Eye   11. Base of the Brain

While holding your student's hands, draw the **Power symbol** in the air above them. Visualize the symbol going into the hands, through the Crown Chakra, to the base of the brain. As you visualize this, silently say the mantra of the symbol three times and tap, once each, at the fingertips over the Crown Chakra (photo 9), the back of the Third Eye (photo 10), and at the base of the brain (photo 11).

12. Return Hands   13. Open Palms

Reach over and return their
hands to their original
position at the heart.

Move to the front and open their
hands out flat with your left
hand underneath.

14. Third Eye

15. Tap into the Palms

16. Pat the Palms

Draw the **Power symbol** over their Third Eye, tapping it in three times while silently saying the mantra. Visualize the symbol going into the Third Eye.

Repeat with the **Mental/Emotional and Distance symbols**.

Draw the **Power symbol** over each of their palms, tapping it in three times while silently saying the mantra. Visualize the symbol moving into each hand.

Using the open palm of your right hand, lightly pat three times into each of the student's open palms.

(NOTE - YOU HAVE ACTIVATED ONLY THE POWER SYMBOL IN THE PALMS)

17. Blow

Return your student's hands to prayer position in front of their heart. In one strong breath blow from your student's hands down toward the Base Chakra, then up to the Third Eye, back down to the Solar Plexus, and then end back at the hands.

18. Affirmation into Heart

Return to the back of your student, putting your hands on their shoulders. Imagine looking down through the student's crown and into their Heart Chakra. See each of the Reiki symbols inside the chakra.

Choose a positive affirmation, such as, **"You are now a powerful and aware Reiki Level I healer."** You are going to place the positive affirmation into their heart. Silently say the affirmation three times with the intention that your student's subconscious accepts it.

19. Sealing

Visualize a triangular door made by placing your thumbs and fingers at the back of your student's head. Silently say to your guides, **"I seal this attunement with love and Divine energy."** (Or use something similar that resonates with you.)

On this door is the Power symbol. See all the symbols inside their head and then visualize this door being closed and sealed. Intend that the process is complete and that your student's direct connection to the Reiki Source and their Reiki guides is now in place.

20. Both Blessed

Once again put your hands on your student's shoulders. Silently say, **"In this attunement we are both blessed."**

21. Raku

Draw the **Raku** lightning bolt down the back to signify banking the fire and separating your aura from your student. You may release the Hui Yin point as you draw the Raku.

Return to the front. Remove their hands from the heart position and lay them, palms down, on the thighs.

State a blessing aloud to let your student know the process is complete.

"You are now a powerful and aware Reiki Level I healer."

23. Thank

Thank your Reiki guides and Masters silently.

BLAJI'S VERSION
SECOND DEGREE ATTUNEMENT – USUI/TIBETAN

This is a combined Usui and Tibetan attunement that passes the sacred symbols from the Usui system as well as the Tibetan Master symbol and includes an attunement to the Third Eye. The Violet Breath is used and the Hui Yin point is held throughout the attunement.

This attunement is given after the symbols have been taught and it aligns the student to their energy, which the student can now access. Through the symbols, the attunement accesses the etheric body more directly as well as empowering the symbols for your student. You will be placing the Power, Distance, and Mental/Emotional symbols into the hands so that they may now be used by the healer. This occurs both when the hands are above the head and in the front with the palms open. All three symbols also go into the Third Eye. The attunement may also stimulate psychic development and intuitive sensitivity.

These are the symbols that you will be passing:

Back – Fire Serpent

Crown – Tibetan Master, Usui Master

Hands Above Crown – Power, Mental/Emotional, Distance

Third Eye – Power, Mental/Emotional, Distance

Open Palms – Power, Mental/Emotional, Distance

Back – Raku

From behind

1. Standing behind your student, draw the **Fire Serpent symbol** starting at the back of your student's head going down to their Base Chakra.

2. Connect energetically by placing your hands over the top of their head, tuning in.

3. Contract and hold the Hui Yin point, keeping your tongue against the alveolar ridge (throughout the entire attunement). Take three Blue Kidney

Breaths to create the Raku energy and then create the **Violet Breath**. Visualize the **Tibetan Master symbol** within the violet light and blow it into the student's head. Visualize the symbol moving from your head, through your breath, into your student's Crown Chakra, and going into the base of their brain. As you visualize this, silently say the mantra of the symbol three times and tap, once each, at the Crown Chakra, the back of the Third Eye, and at the base of the brain.

4. Draw the **Usui Master symbol over your student's head**. Visualize the symbol moving into the Crown Chakra, through the head, to the base of the brain. As you visualize this, silently say the mantra three times and tap, once each, at the Crown Chakra, the back of the Third Eye, and at the base of the brain.

5. Squeeze your student's left shoulder to let them know to raise their hands above their head. If they do not remember to do so, then gently pull up their hands.

6. While **holding your student's hands, draw the Power symbol** in the air above them. Visualize the symbol going into the hands, through the Crown Chakra, to the base of the brain. As you visualize this, silently say the mantra of the symbol three times and tap, once each, at the fingertips over the Crown Chakra, the back of the Third Eye, and at the base of the brain.

7. Repeat step [6], drawing the **Mental/Emotional symbol above the hands.**

8. Repeat step [6], drawing the **Distance symbol above the hands.**

9. Return your student's hands back down to prayer position over the heart.

From the front

1. Go to the front of your student, facing them, and **open their hands** out flat. Place your left hand underneath.

2. Draw the **Power symbol over their Third Eye**, tapping it in three times while silently saying the mantra. Visualize the symbol going into the Third Eye.

3. Repeat step [2], drawing the **Mental/Emotional symbol over the Third Eye.**

4. Repeat step [2], drawing the **Distance symbol over the Third Eye.**

5. Draw the **Power symbol over each of their palms**, tapping it in three times while silently saying the mantra. Visualize the symbol moving into each hand. Then using the open palm of your right hand, lightly pat three times into each of the student's open palms.

6. Repeat step [5], drawing the **Mental/Emotional symbol over each palm.**

7. Repeat step [5], drawing the **Distance symbol over each palm.**

8. Return your student's hands to prayer position in front of their heart. In one strong breath (if you can), blow from your student's hands down toward the Base Chakra, then up to the Third Eye, back down to the Solar Plexus, and then end back at the hands. (If you can keep your Hui Yin point contracted while blowing, that is best. If not, it is ok to release it while you blow and then contract it again.)

From behind

1. Return to the back of your student, putting your hands on their shoulders. Imagine looking down through the student's crown and into their Heart Chakra. See each of the Reiki symbols inside the chakra. Choose a positive affirmation, such as, **"You are now a powerful and aware Reiki Level II practitioner."** You are going to place the positive affirmation into their heart. Silently say the affirmation three times with the intention that your student's subconscious accepts it.

2. Visualize a triangular door made by placing your thumbs and fingers at the back of your student's head. Your thumbs (the base of the triangle) should be at or near the occipital ridge. See all the symbols going inside their head, one by one, and then visualize this door being closed and sealed with the Power symbol on the outside. Silently say to your guides,

"I seal this attunement with love and Divine energy." (Or use something similar that resonates with you.) Intend that the process is complete and that your student's direct connection to the Reiki Source and their Reiki guides is now in place.

3. Once again put your hands on your student's shoulders. Silently say to your guides, "In this attunement we are both blessed."

4. Draw the **Raku** Symbol down the back of your student to seal in the attunement and disconnect your aura from your student's aura. You may release the Hui Yin point as you draw the Raku.

From the front

1. Return to the front, facing your student. Place their hands on their lap, palms facing down. In the case of group attunements, this step is left until all your students have been attuned.

State a blessing aloud to let your student know the process is complete.

"You are now a powerful and aware Reiki Level II practitioner."

ILLUSTRATED ATTUNEMENT – BLAJI LEVEL II

1. Power Up

Protect yourself. Call in your Reiki guides and Masters. Ask the Reiki energy to flow.

2. Fire Serpent

Draw the **Fire Serpent** symbol from the top of their head to the base of the spine.

3. Connect

Place your hands over your student and feel the connection between you.

4. Tibetan Master

Contract and hold the Hui Yin point, keeping your tongue against the alveolar ridge (throughout the entire attunement). Take three Blue Kidney Breaths, and then create the **Violet Breath**. Visualize the **Tibetan Master symbol** within the violet light and blow it into the student's head. Visualize the symbol moving from your head, through your breath, into your student's Crown Chakra, and going into the base of their brain.

As you visualize this, silently say the mantra of the symbol three times and tap, once each, at the Crown Chakra, the back of the Third Eye, and at the base of the brain.

5. Crown	6. Back of the Third Eye	7. Base of the Brain

Draw the **Usui Master symbol over your student's head**. Visualize the symbol moving into the Crown Chakra, through the head, to the base of the brain. As you visualize this, silently say the mantra of the symbol three times and tap, once each, at the Crown Chakra (photo 5), the back of the Third Eye (photo 6), and at the base of the brain (photo 7).

8. Squeeze Shoulder

Squeeze their left shoulder as a signal to raise their hands to the top of their head.

9. Hands Above the Crown   10. Back of the Third Eye   11. Base of the Brain

While holding your student's hands, draw the **Power symbol** in the air above them. Visualize the symbol going into the hands, through the Crown Chakra, to the base of the brain. As you visualize this, silently say the mantra of the symbol three times and tap, once each, at the fingertips over the Crown Chakra (photo 9), the back of the Third Eye (photo 10), and at the base of the brain (photo 11).

Repeat with the **Mental/Emotional, and Distance symbols**.

12. Return Hands   13. Open Palms

Reach over and return their
hands to their original
position at the heart.

Move to the front and open their
hands out flat with your left
hand underneath.

14. Third Eye

Draw the **Power symbol** over their Third Eye, tapping it in three times while silently saying the mantra. Visualize the symbol going into the Third Eye.

Repeat with the **Mental/Emotional and Distance symbols**.

15. Tap into the Palms

Draw the **Power symbol** over each of their palms, tapping it in three times while silently saying the mantra. Visualize the symbol moving into each hand.

16. Pat the Palms

Using the open palm of your right hand, lightly pat three times into each of the student's open palms. This is for the Power symbol. Repeat the whole process tapping (photo 15) and patting (photo 16) with the **Mental/Emotional** and **Distance symbols**.

(NOTE - YOU HAVE ACTIVATED THREE SYMBOLS IN THE PALMS)

17. Blow

Return your student's hands to prayer position in front of their heart. In one strong breath blow from your student's hands down toward the Base Chakra, then up to the Third Eye, back down to the Solar Plexus, and then end back at the hands.

18. Affirmation into Heart

Return to the back of your student, putting your hands on their shoulders. Imagine looking down through the student's crown and into their Heart Chakra. See each of the Reiki symbols inside the chakra.

Choose a positive affirmation, such as, **"You are now a powerful and aware Reiki Level II practitioner."** You are going to place the positive affirmation into their heart. Silently say the affirmation three times with the intention that your student's subconscious accepts it.

19. Sealing

Visualize a triangular door made by placing your thumbs and fingers at the back of your student's head. Silently say to your guides, **"I seal this attunement with love and Divine energy."** (Or use something similar that resonates with you.)

On this door is the Power symbol. See all the symbols inside their head and then visualize this door being closed and sealed. Intend that the process is complete and that your student's direct connection to the Reiki Source and their Reiki guides is now in place.

20. Both Blessed

Place your hands on your student's shoulders. Silently say, "**In this attunement we are both blessed.**"

21. Raku

Draw the **Raku** lightning bolt down the back to signify banking the fire and separating your aura from your student. You may release the Hui Yin point as you draw the Raku.

22. Bless

Return to the front. Remove their hands from the heart position and lay them, palms down, on the thighs.

State a blessing aloud to let your student know the process is complete.

"You are now a powerful and aware Reiki Level II practitioner."

23. Thank

Thank your Reiki guides and Masters silently.

BLAJI'S VERSION
ART/LEVEL III ATTUNEMENT – USUI/TIBETAN

This is a combined Usui and Tibetan attunement that gives the sacred symbols from the Usui system as well as the Tibetan Master symbol and includes an attunement to the Third Eye. The Violet Breath is used and the Hui Yin point is held throughout the attunement. At ART/Level III the Usui Master symbol along with the other three symbols are placed into your student's hands, both when the hands are above the head and in the front with the palms open. The Tibetan Master symbol is not added here, but rather it is added at the Master Level.

These are the symbols that you will be passing:

Back – Fire Serpent

Crown – Tibetan Master

Hands Above Crown – Usui Master, Power, Mental/Emotional, Distance

Third Eye – Usui Master, Power, Mental/Emotional, Distance

Open Palms – Usui Master, Power, Mental/Emotional, Distance

Back – Raku

From behind

1. Standing behind your student, draw the **Fire Serpent symbol** starting at the back of your student's head going down to their Base Chakra.

2. Connect energetically by placing your hands over the top of their head, tuning in.

3. Contract and hold the Hui Yin point, keeping your tongue against the alveolar ridge (throughout the entire attunement). Take three Blue Kidney Breaths to create the Raku energy and then create the **Violet Breath**. Visualize the **Tibetan Master symbol** within the violet light and blow it into the student's head. Visualize the symbol moving from your head, through your breath, into your student's Crown Chakra, and going into the base of their brain. As you visualize this, silently say the mantra of the symbol

three times and tap, once each, at the Crown Chakra, the back of the Third Eye, and at the base of the brain.

4. Squeeze your student's left shoulder to let them know to raise their hands above their head. If they do not remember to do so, then gently pull up their hands.

5. While **holding your student's hands, draw the Usui Master symbol** in the air above them. Visualize the symbol going into the hands, through the Crown Chakra, to the base of the brain. As you visualize this, silently say the mantra of the symbol three times and tap, once each, at the fingertips over the Crown Chakra, the back of the Third Eye, and at the base of the brain.

6. Repeat step [5], drawing the **Power symbol above the hands.**

7. Repeat step [5], drawing the **Mental/Emotional symbol above hands.**

8. Repeat step [5], drawing the **Distance symbol above the hands.**

9. Return your student's hands back down to prayer position over the heart.

From the front

1. Go to the front of your student, facing them, and **open their hands** out flat. Place your left hand underneath.

2. Draw the **Usui Master symbol over their Third Eye**, tapping it in three times while silently saying the mantra. Visualize the symbol going into the Third Eye.

3. Repeat step [2], drawing the **Power symbol over the Third Eye.**

4. Repeat step [2], drawing the **Mental/Emotional symbol over the Third Eye.**

5. Repeat step [2], drawing the **Distance symbol over the Third Eye.**

6. Draw the **Usui Master symbol over each of their palms**, tapping it in three times while silently saying the mantra. Visualize the symbol moving into each hand. Then using the open palm of your right hand, lightly pat three times into each of the student's open palms.

7. Repeat step [6], drawing the **Power symbol over each palm.**

8. Repeat step [6], drawing the **Mental/Emotional symbol over each palm.**

9. Repeat step [6], drawing the **Distance symbol over each palm.**

10. Return your student's hands to prayer position in front of their heart. In one strong breath (if you can), blow from your student's hands down toward the Base Chakra, then up to the Third Eye, back down to the Solar Plexus, and then end back at the hands. (If you can keep your Hui Yin point contracted while blowing, that is best. If not, it is ok to release it while you blow and then contract it again.)

From behind

1. Return to the back of your student, putting your hands on their shoulders. Imagine looking down through the student's crown and into their Heart Chakra. See each of the Reiki symbols inside the chakra. Choose a positive affirmation, such as, **"You are now a powerful and aware Reiki Level III practitioner."** You are going to place the positive affirmation into their heart. Silently say the affirmation three times with the intention that your student's subconscious accepts it.

2. Visualize a triangular door made by placing your thumbs and fingers at the back of your student's head. Your thumbs (the base of the triangle) should be at or near the occipital ridge. See all the symbols going inside their head, one by one, and then visualize this door being closed and sealed with the Power symbol on the outside. Silently say to your guides, **"I seal this attunement with love and Divine energy."** (Or use something similar that resonates with you.) Intend that the process is complete and that your student's direct connection to the Reiki Source and their Reiki guides is now in place.

3. Once again put your hands on your student's shoulders. Silently say to your guides, **"In this attunement we are both blessed."**

4. Draw the **Raku** Symbol down the back of your student to seal in the attunement and disconnect your aura from your student's aura. You may release the Hui Yin point as you draw the Raku.

From the front

1. Return to the front, facing your student. Place their hands on their lap, palms facing down. In the case of group attunements, this step is left until all your students have been attuned.

   State a blessing aloud to let your student know the process is complete.

   "You are now a powerful and aware Reiki Level III practitioner."

ILLUSTRATED ATTUNEMENT – BLAJI ART/LEVEL III

1. Power Up

Protect yourself. Call in your Reiki guides and Masters. Ask the Reiki energy to flow.

2. Fire Serpent

Draw the **Fire Serpent** symbol from the top of their head to the base of the spine.

3. Connect

Place your hands over your student and feel the connection between you.

4. Tibetan Master

Contract and hold the Hui Yin point, keeping your tongue against the alveolar ridge (throughout the entire attunement). Take three Blue Kidney Breaths, and then create the **Violet Breath**. Visualize the **Tibetan Master symbol** within the violet light and blow it into the student's head. Visualize the symbol moving from your head, through your breath, into your student's Crown Chakra, and going into the base of their brain.

As you visualize this, silently say the mantra of the symbol three times and tap, once each, at the Crown Chakra, the back of the Third Eye, and at the base of the brain.

5. Crown	6. Back of the Third Eye	7. Base of the Brain

Draw the **Usui Master symbol over your student's head**. Visualize the symbol moving into the Crown Chakra, through the head, to the base of the brain. As you visualize this, silently say the mantra of the symbol three times and tap, once each, at the Crown Chakra (photo 5), the back of the Third Eye (photo 6), and at the base of the brain (photo 7).

Repeat with the **Power, Mental/Emotional, and Distance symbols**.

8. Squeeze Shoulder

Squeeze their left shoulder as a signal to raise their hands to the top of their head.

9. Hands Above the Crown   10. Back of the Third Eye   11. Base of the Brain

While holding your student's hands, draw the **Usui Master symbol** in the air above them. Visualize the symbol going into the hands, through the Crown Chakra, to the base of the brain. As you visualize this, silently say the mantra of the symbol three times and tap, once each, at the fingertips over the Crown Chakra (photo 9), the back of the Third Eye (photo 10), and at the base of the brain (photo 11).

Repeat with the **Power, Mental/Emotional, and Distance symbols**.

12. Return Hands   13. Open Palms

Reach over and return their   Move to the front and open their
hands to their original   hands out flat with your left
position at the heart.   hand underneath.

14. Third Eye

Draw the **Usui Master symbol** over their Third Eye, tapping it in three times while silently saying the mantra. Visualize the symbol going into the Third Eye.

Repeat with the **Power, Mental/Emotional, and Distance symbols.**

15. Tap into the Palms

Draw the **Usui Master symbol** over each of their palms, tapping it in three times while silently saying the mantra. Visualize the symbol moving into each hand.

16. Pat the Palms

Using the open palm of your right hand, lightly pat three times into each of the student's open palms. This is for the Usui Master symbol. Repeat the whole process tapping (photo 15) and patting (photo 16) with the **Power, Mental/Emotional, and Distance symbols.**

(NOTE - YOU HAVE ACTIVATED FOUR SYMBOLS IN THE PALMS)

17. Blow

Return your student's hands to prayer position in front of their heart. In one strong breath blow from your student's hands down toward the Base Chakra, then up to the Third Eye, back down to the Solar Plexus, and then end back at the hands.

18. Affirmation into Heart

Return to the back of your student, putting your hands on their shoulders. Imagine looking down through the student's crown and into their Heart Chakra. See each of the Reiki symbols inside the chakra.

Choose a positive affirmation, such as, **"You are now a powerful and aware Reiki Level III practitioner."** You are going to place the positive affirmation into their heart. Silently say the affirmation three times with the intention that your student's subconscious accepts it.

19. Sealing

Visualize a triangular door made by placing your thumbs and fingers at the back of your student's head. Silently say to your guides, **"I seal this attunement with love and Divine energy."** (Or use something similar that resonates with you.)

On this door is the Power symbol. See all the symbols inside their head and then visualize this door being closed and sealed. Intend that the process is complete and that your student's direct connection to the Reiki Source and their Reiki guides is now in place.

20. Both Blessed

Place your hands on your student's shoulders. Silently say, **"In this attunement we are both blessed."**

21. Raku

Draw the **Raku** lightning bolt down the back to signify banking the fire and separating your aura from your student. You may release the Hui Yin point as you draw the Raku.

22. Bless

Return to the front. Remove their hands from the heart position and lay them, palms down, on the thighs.

State a blessing aloud to let your student know the process is complete.

"You are now a powerful and aware Reiki Level III practitioner."

23. Thank

Thank your Reiki guides and Masters silently.

BLAJI'S VERSION
MASTER ATTUNEMENT – USUI/TIBETAN

This is a combined Usui and Tibetan attunement that gives the sacred symbols from the Usui system as well as the Tibetan Master symbol and includes an attunement to the Third Eye. The Violet Breath is used and the Hui Yin point is held throughout the attunement. In this Master attunement you are placing all six symbols into the hands, both when the hands are above the head and in the front with the palms open. The Tibetan Master symbol is passed through the Violet Breath into the hands when the hands are above the head.

These are the symbols that you will be passing:

Back – Fire Serpent

Hands Above Crown – Tibetan Master, Fire Serpent, Usui Master, Power, Mental/Emotional, Distance

Third Eye – Tibetan Master, Fire Serpent, Usui Master, Power, Mental/Emotional, Distance

Open Palms – Tibetan Master, Fire Serpent, Usui Master, Power, Mental/Emotional, Distance

Back – Raku

From behind

1. Standing behind your student, draw the **Fire Serpent symbol** starting at the back of your student's head going down to their Base Chakra.

2. Connect energetically by placing your hands over the top of their head, tuning in.

3. Squeeze your student's left shoulder to let them know to raise their hands above their head. If they do not remember to do so, then gently pull up their hands.

4. Contract and hold the Hui Yin point, keeping your tongue against the

alveolar ridge (throughout the entire attunement). Take three Blue Kidney Breaths to create the Raku energy and then create the **Violet Breath**. Visualize the **Tibetan Master symbol** within the violet light and blow it into the student's fingertips above their head. Visualize the symbol moving from your head, through your breath, into your student's Crown Chakra, and going into the base of their brain. As you visualize this, silently say the mantra of the symbol three times and tap, once each, at the fingertips, the back of the Third Eye, and at the base of the brain.

5. While **holding your student's hands, draw the Fire Serpent symbol** in the air above them. Visualize the symbol going into the hands, through the Crown Chakra, to the base of the brain. As you visualize this, silently say the mantra of the symbol three times and tap, once each, at the fingertips over the Crown Chakra, the back of the Third Eye, and at the base of the brain.

6. Repeat step [5], drawing the **Usui Master symbol above the hands.**

7. Repeat step [5], drawing the **Power symbol above the hands.**

8. Repeat step [5], drawing the **Mental/Emotional symbol above the hands.**

9. Repeat step [5], drawing the **Distance symbol above the hands.**

10. Return your student's hands back down to prayer position over the heart.

From the front

1. Go to the front of your student, facing them, and **open their hands** out flat. Place your left hand underneath.

2. Create the **Tibetan Master symbol** with the Violet Breath and blow it into the **Third Eye**, tapping it in three times while silently saying the mantra. Visualize the symbol going into the Third Eye.

3. Draw the **Fire Serpent symbol over the Third Eye**, tapping it in three times while silently saying the mantra. Visualize the symbol going into their Third Eye.

4. Repeat step [3], drawing the **Usui Master symbol over the Third Eye.**

5. Repeat step [3], drawing the **Power symbol over the Third Eye.**

6. Repeat step [3], drawing the **Mental/Emotional symbol over Third Eye.**

7. Repeat step [3], drawing the **Distance symbol over the Third Eye.**

8. Create the **Tibetan Master symbol** with the Violet Breath and blow it into **each of their palms**, tapping it in three times while silently saying the mantra. Visualize the symbol moving into each hand. Then using the open palm of your right hand, lightly pat three times into each of the student's open palms.

9. Draw the **Fire Serpent symbol over the palms**, tapping it in three times while silently saying the mantra. Visualize the symbol moving into each hand. Then using the open palm of your right hand, lightly pat three times into each of the student's open palms.

10. Repeat step [9], drawing the **Usui Master symbol over the palms.**

11. Repeat step [9], drawing the **Power symbol over the palms.**

12. Repeat step [9], drawing the **Mental/Emotional symbol over the palms.**

13. Repeat step [9], drawing the **Distance symbol over the palms.**

14. Return your student's hands to prayer position in front of their heart. In one strong breath (if you can), blow from your student's hands down toward the Base Chakra, then up to the Third Eye, back down to the Solar Plexus, and then end back at the hands. (If you can keep your Hui Yin point contracted while blowing, that is best. If not, it is ok to release it while you blow and then contract it again.)

From behind

1. Return to the back of your student, putting your hands on their shoulders. Imagine looking down through the student's crown and into their Heart Chakra. See each of the Reiki symbols inside the chakra. Choose a positive affirmation, such as, **"You are now a powerful and aware Reiki Master."** You are

going to place the positive affirmation into their heart. Silently say the affirmation three times with the intention that your student's subconscious accepts it.

2. Visualize a triangular door made by placing your thumbs and fingers at the back of your student's head. Your thumbs (the base of the triangle) should be at or near the occipital ridge. See all the symbols going inside their head, one by one, and then visualize this door being closed and sealed with the Power symbol on the outside. Silently say to your guides, **"I seal this attunement with love and Divine energy."** (Or use something similar that resonates with you.) Intend that the process is complete and that your student's direct connection to the Reiki Source and their Reiki guides is now in place.

3. Once again put your hands on your student's shoulders. Silently say to your guides, **"In this attunement we are both blessed."**

4. Draw the **Raku** Symbol down the back of your student to seal in the attunement and disconnect your aura from your student's aura. You may release the Hui Yin point as you draw the Raku.

From the front

1. Return to the front, facing your student. Place their hands on their lap, palms facing down. In the case of group attunements, this step is left until all your students have been attuned.

State a blessing aloud to let your student know the process is complete.

"You are now a powerful and aware Reiki Master."

ILLUSTRATED ATTUNEMENT – BLAJI MASTERS

1. Power Up

Protect yourself. Call in your Reiki guides and Masters. Ask the Reiki energy to flow.

2. Fire Serpent

Draw the **Fire Serpent** symbol from the top of their head to the base of the spine.

3. Connect

Place your hands over your student and feel the connection between you.

4. Squeeze Shoulder

Squeeze their left shoulder as a signal to raise their hands to the top of their head.

5. Tibetan Master over the Hands

Contract and hold the Hui Yin point, keeping your tongue against the alveolar ridge (throughout the entire attunement). Take three Blue Kidney Breaths, and then create the **Violet Breath.** Visualize the **Tibetan Master symbol** within the violet light and blow it into the student's fingertips. Visualize the symbol moving through their hands and the Crown Chakra and going into the base of their brain.

As you visualize this, silently say the mantra of the symbol three times and tap, once each, at the finger tips over the Crown Chakra, the back of the Third Eye, and at the base of the brain.

6. Hands Above the Crown	7. Back of the Third Eye	8. Base of the Brain

While holding your student's hands, draw the **Fire Serpent symbol** in the air above them. Visualize the symbol going into the hands, through the Crown Chakra, to the base of the brain. As you visualize this, silently say the mantra of the symbol three times and tap, once each, at the fingertips over the Crown Chakra (photo 6), the back of the Third Eye (photo 7), and at the base of the brain (photo 8).

Repeat with the **Usui Master, Power, Mental/Emotional, and Distance symbols.**

9. Return Hands

Reach over and return their
hands to their original
position at the heart.

10. Open Palms

Move to the front and open their
hands out flat with your left
hand underneath.

11. Third Eye

Create the **Tibetan Master symbol** with the Violet
Breath and blow it into the Third Eye, tapping it in
three times while silently saying the mantra.
Visualize the symbol going into the Third Eye.

Draw the following symbols in order over the Third
Eye, tapping them in three times, while silently
saying their mantra. **Fire Serpent, Usui Master, Power,
Mental/Emotional, and Distance symbols**. Visualize each
symbol going into the Third Eye.

12. Tap into the Palms

Create the **Tibetan Master symbol** with the Violet Breath and blow it into each palm, tapping it in three times while silently saying the mantra. Visualize the symbol moving into each hand.

13. Pat the Palms

Using the open palm of your right hand, lightly pat three times into each of the student's open palms. This is done after each individual symbol is drawn (or blown in for the Tibetan Master).

For the following symbols in order: **Fire Serpent, Usui Master, Power, Mental/Emotional, and Distance symbol,** you are going to draw (not blow in), then tap (photo 12) and pat (photo 13) each one individually into the palms.

(NOTE - YOU HAVE ACTIVATED ALL THE SYMBOLS IN THE PALMS)

14. Blow

Return your student's hands to prayer position in front of their heart. In one strong breath blow from your student's hands down toward the Base Chakra, then up to the Third Eye, back down to the Solar Plexus, and then end back at the hands.

15. Affirmation into Heart

Return to the back of your student, putting your hands on their shoulders. Imagine looking down through the student's crown and into their Heart Chakra. See each of the Reiki symbols inside the chakra.

Choose a positive affirmation, such as, **"You are now a powerful and aware Reiki Master."** You are going to place the positive affirmation into their heart. Silently say the affirmation three times with the intention that your student's subconscious accepts it.

16. Sealing

Visualize a triangular door made by placing your thumbs and fingers at the back of your student's head. Silently say to your guides, **"I seal this attunement with love and Divine energy."** (Or use something similar that resonates with you.)

On this door is the Power symbol. See all the symbols inside their head and then visualize this door being closed and sealed. Intend that the process is complete and that your student's direct connection to the Reiki Source and their Reiki guides is now in place..

17. Both Blessed	18. Raku

Place your hands on your student's shoulders. Silently say, **"In this attunement we are both blessed."**	Draw the **Raku** lightning bolt down the back to signify banking the fire and separating your aura from your student. You may release the Hui Yin point as you draw the Raku.

19. Bless

Return to the front. Remove their hands from the heart position and lay them, palms down, on the thighs.

State a blessing aloud to let your student know the process is complete

"You are now a powerful and aware Reiki Master."

20. Thank

Thank your Reiki guides and Masters silently.

ALTERNATIVE INITIATORY ATTUNEMENT

On the following pages are the Usui attunements (long version) and the Tibetan attunements. I personally prefer to use the Blaji attunements for my Reiki initiatory (level) attunements. The other versions are here for your consideration. If you feel you resonate better with these versions of the attunements, by all means use them.

CHAPTER 12
USUI SYSTEM INITIATORY ATTUNEMENTS

FIRST DEGREE ATTUNEMENT – USUI SYSTEM – LONG VERSION

This is the Western/Takata system, which does not use the Tibetan symbols or the Violet Breath. This Level I attunement is given in four stages that focus on raising the vibration of the energy in the physical body and opening the upper chakras. You will only be placing the Power symbol into the hands. This is done when the hands are above the Crown Chakra and when they are open in front.

The symbols that you will be passing:

Crown – Usui Master, Distance, Mental/Emotional

Hands Above Crown – Power

Third Eye – Power, Mental/Emotional, Distance

Open Palms – Power

STAGE 1

From behind

1. Stand behind your student. Connect energetically by placing your hands over the top of their head, tuning in.

2. Draw the **Usui Master symbol over the head.** Visualize the symbol going into the Crown Chakra and continuing through the head to the base of the brain. As you visualize this, silently say the mantra of the symbol three times and tap, once each, at the Crown Chakra, the back of the Third Eye Chakra, and at the base of the brain.

3. Squeeze your student's left shoulder to let them know to raise their hands above their head. If they do not remember to do so, then gently pull up their hands.

4. While **holding your student's hands, draw the Power symbol** in the air above them. Visualize the symbol going into the hands, through the Crown Chakra, to the base of the brain. As you visualize this, silently say the mantra of the symbol three times and tap, once each, at the fingertips over the Crown Chakra, the back of the Third Eye, and at the base of the brain.

5. Return your student's hands back down to prayer position over the heart.

From the front

1. Go to the front of your student, facing them, and **open their hands** out flat. Place your left hand underneath.

2. Draw the **Power symbol over their Third Eye**, tapping it in three times while silently saying the mantra. Visualize the symbol going into the Third Eye.

3. Draw the **Power symbol over each of their palms**, tapping it in three times while silently saying the mantra. Visualize the symbol moving into each hand. Then using the open palm of your right hand, lightly pat three times into each of the student's open palms.

4. Return your student's hands to prayer position in front of their heart. In one strong breath (if you can), blow from your student's hands down toward the Base Chakra, then up to the Third Eye, back down to the Solar Plexus, and then end back at the hands.

From behind

1. Return to the back of your student, putting your hands on their shoulders. Imagine looking down through the student's crown and into their Heart Chakra. See each of the Reiki symbols inside the chakra. Choose a positive affirmation, such as, **"You are now a powerful and aware Reiki Level I healer."** You are going to place the positive affirmation into their heart. Silently say the affirmation three times with the intention that your student's subconscious accepts it.

2. Visualize a triangular door made by placing your thumbs and fingers at the back of your student's head. Your thumbs (the base of the triangle) should be at or near the occipital ridge. See all the symbols going inside their head, one by one, and then visualize this door being closed and sealed with the Power symbol on the outside. Silently say to your guides, **"I seal this attunement with love and Divine energy."** (Or use something similar that resonates with you.) Intend that the process is complete and that your student's direct connection to the Reiki Source and their Reiki guides is now in place.

3. Once again put your hands on your student's shoulders. Silently say to your guides, **"In this attunement we are both blessed."**

From the front

1. Return to the front, facing your student. Place their hands on their lap, palms facing down. In the case of group attunements, this step is left until all your students have been attuned.

STAGE 2
(NOTE – THIS IS THE SAME AS STAGE 1 BUT ADDING THE DISTANCE SYMBOL)

From behind

1. Stand behind your student. Connect energetically by placing your hands over the top of their head, tuning in.

2. Draw the **Usui Master symbol over the head.** Visualize the symbol going into the Crown Chakra and continuing through the head to the base of the brain. As you visualize this, silently say the mantra of the symbol three times and tap, once each, at the Crown Chakra, the back of the Third Eye Chakra, and at the base of the brain.

3. Repeat step (2) using the **Distance symbol**.

4. Squeeze your student's left shoulder to let them know to raise their hands above their head. If they do not remember to do so, then gently pull up their hands.

5. While **holding your student's hands, draw the Power symbol** in the air above them. Visualize the symbol going into the hands, through the Crown Chakra, to the base of the brain. As you visualize this, silently say the mantra of the symbol three times and tap, once each, at the fingertips over the Crown Chakra, the back of the Third Eye, and at the base of the brain.

6. Return your student's hands back down to prayer position over the heart.

From the front

1. Go to the front of your student, facing them, and **open their hands** out flat. Place your left hand underneath.

2. Draw the **Power symbol over their Third Eye**, tapping it in three times while silently saying the mantra. Visualize the symbol going into the Third Eye.

3. Repeat step [2] using the **Distance symbol.**

4. Draw the **Power symbol over each of their palms**, tapping it in three times while silently saying the mantra. Visualize the symbol moving into

each hand. Then using the open palm of your right hand, lightly pat three times into each of the student's open palms.

5. Return your student's hands to prayer position in front of their heart. In one strong breath (if you can), blow from your student's hands down toward the Base Chakra, then up to the Third Eye, back down to the Solar Plexus, and then end back at the hands.

From behind

1. Return to the back of your student, putting your hands on their shoulders. Imagine looking down through the student's crown and into their Heart Chakra. See each of the Reiki symbols inside the chakra. Choose a positive affirmation, such as, **"You are now a powerful and aware Reiki Level I healer."** You are going to place the positive affirmation into their heart. Silently say the affirmation three times with the intention that your student's subconscious accepts it.

2. Visualize a triangular door made by placing your thumbs and fingers at the back of your student's head. Your thumbs (the base of the triangle) should be at or near the occipital ridge. Silently say to your guides, **"I seal this attunement with love and Divine energy."** (Or use something similar that resonates with you.) On this door is the Power symbol. See all the symbols inside their head and then visualize this door being closed and sealed. Intend that the process is complete and that your student's direct connection to the Reiki Source and their Reiki guides is now in place.

3. Once again put your hands on your student's shoulders. Silently say to your guides, **"In this attunement we are both blessed."**

From the front

1. Return to the front, facing your student. Place their hands on their lap, palms facing down. In the case of group attunements, this step is left until all your students have been attuned.

STAGE 3
(NOTE – THIS IS THE EXACT SAME AS STAGE 2)

From behind

1. Stand behind your student. Connect energetically by placing your hands over the top of their head, tuning in.

2. Draw the **Usui Master symbol over the head.** Visualize the symbol going into the Crown Chakra and continuing through the head to the base of the brain. As you visualize this, silently say the mantra of the symbol three times and tap, once each, at the Crown Chakra, the back of the Third Eye Chakra, and at the base of the brain.

3. Repeat step [2] using the **Distance symbol**.

4. Squeeze your student's left shoulder to let them know to raise their hands above their head. If they do not remember to do so, then gently pull up their hands.

5. While **holding your student's hands, draw the Power symbol** in the air above them. Visualize the symbol going into the hands, through the Crown Chakra, to the base of the brain. As you visualize this, silently say the mantra of the symbol three times and tap, once each, at the fingertips over the Crown Chakra, the back of the Third Eye, and at the base of the brain.

6. Return your student's hands back down to prayer position over the heart.

From the front

1. Go to the front of your student, facing them, and **open their hands** out flat. Place your left hand underneath.

2. Draw the **Power symbol over their Third Eye**, tapping it in three times while silently saying the mantra. Visualize the symbol going into the Third Eye.

3. Repeat step [2] using the **Distance symbol.**

4. Draw the **Power symbol over each of their palms**, tapping it in three times while silently saying the mantra. Visualize the symbol moving into

each hand. Then using the open palm of your right hand, lightly pat three times into each of the student's open palms.

5. Return your student's hands to prayer position in front of their heart. In one strong breath (if you can), blow from your student's hands down toward the Base Chakra, then up to the Third Eye, back down to the Solar Plexus, and then end back at the hands.

From behind

1. Return to the back of your student, putting your hands on their shoulders. Imagine looking down through the student's crown and into their Heart Chakra. See each of the Reiki symbols inside the chakra. Choose a positive affirmation, such as, **"You are now a powerful and aware Reiki Level I healer."** You are going to place the positive affirmation into their heart. Silently say the affirmation three times with the intention that your student's subconscious accepts it.

2. Visualize a triangular door made by placing your thumbs and fingers at the back of your student's head. Your thumbs (the base of the triangle) should be at or near the occipital ridge. See all the symbols going inside their head, one by one, and then visualize this door being closed and sealed with the Power symbol on the outside. Silently say to your guides, **"I seal this attunement with love and Divine energy."** (Or use something similar that resonates with you.) Intend that the process is complete and that your student's direct connection to the Reiki Source and their Reiki guides is now in place.

3. Once again put your hands on your student's shoulders. Silently say to your guides, **"In this attunement we are both blessed."**

From the front

1. Return to the front, facing your student. Place their hands on their lap, palms facing down. In the case of group attunements, this step is left

until all your students have been attuned.

STAGE 4
(NOTE – THIS IS THE SAME AS STAGE 1, BUT ADDING THE DISTANCE SYMBOL & THE MENTAL/EMOTIONAL SYMBOL)

From behind

1. Stand behind your student. Connect energetically by placing your hands over the top of their head, tuning in.

2. Draw the **Usui Master symbol over the head.** Visualize the symbol going into the Crown Chakra and continuing through the head to the base of the brain. As you visualize this, silently say the mantra of the symbol three times and tap, once each, at the Crown Chakra, the back of the Third Eye Chakra, and at the base of the brain.

3. Repeat step [2] using the **Mental/Emotional symbol**.

4. Repeat step [2] using the **Distance symbol**.

5. Squeeze your student's left shoulder to let them know to raise their hands above their head. If they do not remember to do so, then gently pull up their hands.

6. While **holding your student's hands, draw the Power symbol** in the air above them. Visualize the symbol going into the hands, through the Crown Chakra, to the base of the brain. As you visualize this, silently say the mantra of the symbol three times and tap, once each, at the fingertips over the Crown Chakra, the back of the Third Eye, and at the base of the brain.

7. Return your student's hands back down to prayer position over the heart.

From the front

1. Go to the front of your student, facing them, and **open their hands** out flat. Place your left hand underneath.

2. Draw the **Power symbol over their Third Eye**, tapping it in three times while silently saying the mantra. Visualize the symbol going into the Third Eye.

3. Repeat step [2] using the **Mental/Emotional symbol**.

4. Repeat step [2] using the **Distance symbol**.

5. Draw the **Power symbol over each of their palms**, tapping it in three times while silently saying the mantra. Visualize the symbol moving into each hand. Then using the open palm of your right hand, lightly pat three times into each of the student's open palms.

6. Return your student's hands to prayer position in front of their heart. In one strong breath (if you can), blow from your student's hands down toward the Base Chakra, then up to the Third Eye, back down to the Solar Plexus, and then end back at the hands.

From behind

1. Return to the back of your student, putting your hands on their shoulders. Imagine looking down through the student's crown and into their Heart Chakra. See each of the Reiki symbols inside the chakra. Choose a positive affirmation, such as, **"You are now a powerful and aware Reiki Level I healer."** You are going to place the positive affirmation into their heart. Silently say the affirmation three times with the intention that your student's subconscious accepts it.

2. Visualize a triangular door made by placing your thumbs and fingers at the back of your student's head. Your thumbs (the base of the triangle) should be at or near the occipital ridge. Silently say to your guides, **"I seal this attunement with love and Divine energy."** (Or use something similar that resonates with you.) On this door is the Power symbol. See all the symbols inside their head and then visualize this door being closed and sealed. Intend that the process is complete and that your student's direct connection to the Reiki Source and their Reiki guides is now in place.

3. Once again put your hands on your student's shoulders. Silently say to your guides, **"In this attunement we are both blessed."**

From the front

1. Return to the front, facing your student. Place their hands on their lap, palms facing down. In the case of group attunements, this step is left until all your students have been attuned.

   State a blessing aloud to let your student know the process is complete.

*"You are now a powerful and aware
Reiki Level I healer."*

SECOND DEGREE ATTUNEMENT – USUI SYSTEM – LONG VERSION

This is the Western/Takata system, which does not use the Tibetan symbols or the Violet Breath. The attunement is given after the symbols have been taught. You will be placing the Power, Distance, and Mental/Emotional symbols into the hands so that they may now be used by the healer. This occurs both when the hands are above the head and in the front with the palms open. All three symbols also go into the Third Eye. The attunement may also stimulate psychic development and intuitive sensitivity.

The symbols that you will be passing:

Crown – Usui Master

Hands Above Crown – Power, Mental/Emotional, Distance

Third Eye – Power, Mental/Emotional, Distance

Open Palms – Power, Mental/Emotional, Distance

From behind

1. Stand behind your student. Connect energetically by placing your hands over the top of their head, tuning in.

2. Draw the **Usui Master symbol over the head.** Visualize the symbol going into the Crown Chakra and continuing through the head to the base of the brain. As you visualize this, silently say the mantra of the symbol three times and tap, once each, at the Crown Chakra, the back of the Third Eye Chakra, and at the base of the brain.

3. Squeeze your student's left shoulder to let them know to raise their hands above their head. If they do not remember to do so, then gently pull up their hands.

4. While **holding your student's hands, draw the Power symbol** in the air above them. Visualize the symbol going into the hands, through the Crown Chakra, to the base of the brain. As you visualize this, silently say the mantra of the symbol three times and tap, once each, at the fingertips over the Crown Chakra, the back of the Third Eye, and at the base of the brain.

5. Repeat step [4] using the **Mental/Emotional symbol**.

6. Repeat step [4] using the **Distance symbol**.

7. Return your student's hands back down to prayer position over the heart.

From the front

1. Go to the front of your student, facing them, and **open their hands** out flat. Place your left hand underneath.

2. Draw the **Power symbol over their Third Eye**, tapping it in three times while silently saying the mantra. Visualize the symbol going into the Third Eye.

3. Repeat step [2] using the **Mental/Emotional symbol**.

4. Repeat step [2] using the **Distance symbol**.

5. Draw the **Power symbol over each of their palms**, tapping it in three times while silently saying the mantra. Visualize the symbol moving into each hand. Then using the open palm of your right hand, lightly pat three times into each of the student's open palms.

6. Repeat step [5] using the **Mental/Emotional symbol**.

7. Repeat step [5] using the **Distance symbol**.

8. Return your student's hands to prayer position in front of their heart. In one strong breath (if you can), blow from your student's hands down toward the Base Chakra, then up to the Third Eye, back down to the Solar Plexus, and then end back at the hands.

From behind

1. Return to the back of your student, putting your hands on their shoulders. Imagine looking down through the student's crown and into their Heart Chakra. See each of the Reiki symbols inside the chakra. Choose a positive affirmation, such as, **"You are now a powerful and aware Reiki Level II practitioner."** You are going to place the positive affirmation into their heart. Silently say the affirmation three times with the intention that your student's subconscious accepts it.

2. Visualize a triangular door made by placing your thumbs and fingers at the back of your student's head. Your thumbs (the base of the triangle) should be at or near the occipital ridge. See all the symbols going inside their head, one by one, and then visualize this door being closed and sealed with the Power symbol on the outside. Silently say to your guides, **"I seal this attunement with love and Divine energy."** (Or use something similar that resonates with you.) Intend that the process is complete and that your student's direct connection to the Reiki Source and their Reiki guides is now in place.

3. Once again put your hands on your student's shoulders. Silently say to your guides, **"In this attunement we are both blessed."**

From the front

1. Return to the front, facing your student. Place their hands on their lap, palms facing down. In the case of group attunements, this step is left until all your students have been attuned.

State a blessing aloud to let your student know the process is complete.

*"You are now a powerful and aware
Reiki Level II practitioner."*

ART/LEVEL III ATTUNEMENT – USUI SYSTEM – LONG VERSION

This is the Western/Takata system, which does not use the Tibetan symbols or the Violet Breath. There is only one attunement after Level II, which is given at Advanced Reiki Training (ART)/Level III. Even though this is called the Level III attunement, it is attuning you to the Usui Master symbol (the Master course is simply how to pass attunements and teach Reiki). It is given after the Master symbol has been taught and it aligns the student to the symbol's energy which they can now access. You will be placing all four symbols (Power, Distance, Mental/Emotional, and Usui Master) into the hands, both above the head and into the open palms. You will also place all four symbols into the Third Eye.

The symbols that you will be passing:

Crown – None

Hands Above Crown – Usui Master, Power, Mental/Emotional, Distance

Third Eye – Usui Master, Power, Mental/Emotional, Distance

Open Palms – Usui Master, Power, Mental/Emotional, Distance

From behind

1. Stand behind your student. Connect energetically by placing your hands over the top of their head, tuning in.

2. Squeeze your student's left shoulder to let them know to raise their hands above their head. If they do not remember to do so, then gently pull up their hands.

3. While **holding your student's hands, draw the Power symbol** in the air above them. Visualize the symbol going into the hands, through the Crown Chakra, to the base of the brain. As you visualize this, silently say the mantra of the symbol three times and tap, once each, at the fingertips over the Crown Chakra, the back of the Third Eye, and at the base of the brain.

4. Repeat step [3] using the **Power symbol**.

5. Repeat step [3] using the **Mental/Emotional symbol**.

6. Repeat step [3] using the **Distance symbol**.

7. Return your student's hands back down to prayer position over the heart.

From the front

1. Go to the front of your student, facing them, and **open their hands** out flat. Place your left hand underneath.

2. Draw the **Usui Master symbol over their Third Eye**, tapping it in three times while silently saying the mantra. Visualize the symbol going into the Third Eye.

3. Repeat step [2] using the **Power symbol**.

4. Repeat step [2] using the **Mental/Emotional symbol**.

5. Repeat step [2] using the **Distance symbol**.

6. Draw the **Usui Master symbol over each of their palms**, tapping it in three times while silently saying the mantra. Visualize the symbol moving into each hand. Then using the open palm of your right hand, lightly pat three times into each of the student's open palms.

7. Repeat step [6] using the **Power symbol**.

8. Repeat step [6] using the **Mental/Emotional symbol**.

9. Repeat step [6] using the **Distance symbol**.

10. In one strong breath (if you can), blow from your student's hands down toward the Base Chakra, then up to the Third Eye, back down to the Solar Plexus, and then end back at the hands.

From behind

1. Return to the back of your student, putting your hands on their shoulders. Imagine looking down through the student's crown and into their Heart Chakra. See each of the Reiki symbols inside the chakra. Choose a positive affirmation, such as, **"You are now a powerful and aware advanced**

Reiki practitioner." You are going to place the positive affirmation into their heart. Silently say the affirmation three times with the intention that your student's subconscious accepts it.

2. Visualize a triangular door made by placing your thumbs and fingers at the back of your student's head. Your thumbs (the base of the triangle) should be at or near the occipital ridge. See all the symbols going inside their head, one by one, and then visualize this door being closed and sealed with the Power symbol on the outside. Silently say to your guides, **"I seal this attunement with love and Divine energy."** (Or use something similar that resonates with you.) Intend that the process is complete and that your student's direct connection to the Reiki Source and their Reiki guides is now in place.

3. Once again put your hands on your student's shoulders. Silently say to your guides, **"In this attunement we are both blessed."**

From the front

1. Return to the front, facing your student. Place their hands on their lap, palms facing down. In the case of group attunements, this step is left until all your students have been attuned.

   State a blessing aloud to let your student know the process is complete.

*"You are now a powerful and aware
advanced Reiki practitioner."*

CHAPTER 13

TIBETAN SYSTEM INITIATORY ATTUNEMENTS

FIRST DEGREE ATTUNEMENT – TIBETAN

The following is the long version of the Level I Tibetan attunement which is given in four stages. Although many Masters believe that stage four is the only one necessary for the attunement as it contains all the elements of the other three stages. The symbols are not placed into the Third Eye. The Violet Breath is used and the Hui Yin point is held throughout the attunement.

These are the symbols that you will be passing:

Back – Fire Serpent

Crown – Tibetan Master, Usui Master, Mental/Emotional, Distance

Hands Above Crown – Power

Open Palms – Power

STAGE 1

From behind

1. Standing behind your student, draw the **Fire Serpent symbol** starting at the back of your student's head going down to their Base Chakra.

2. Connect energetically by placing your hands over the top of their head, tuning in.

3. Contract and hold the Hui Yin point, keeping your tongue against the alveolar ridge (throughout the entire attunement). Take three Blue Kidney Breaths to create the Raku energy and then create the **Violet Breath**. Visualize the **Tibetan Master symbol** within the violet light and blow it into the student's head. Visualize the symbol moving from your head, through your breath, into your student's Crown Chakra, and going into the base of their brain. As you visualize this, silently say the mantra of the symbol three times and tap, once each, at the Crown Chakra, the back of the Third Eye, and at the base of the brain.

4. Draw the **Usui Master symbol over your student's head**. Visualize the symbol moving into the Crown Chakra, through the head, to the base of the brain. As you visualize this, silently say the mantra of the symbol three times and tap, once each, at the Crown Chakra, the back of the Third Eye, and at the base of the brain.

5. Squeeze your student's left shoulder to let them know to raise their hands above their head. If they do not remember to do so, then gently pull up their hands.

6. While **holding your student's hands, draw the Power symbol** in the air above them. Visualize the symbol going into the hands, through the Crown Chakra, to the base of the brain. As you visualize this, silently say the mantra of the symbol three times and tap, once each, at the fingertips over the Crown Chakra, the back of the Third Eye, and at the base of the brain.

7. Return your student's hands back down to prayer position over the heart.

From the front

1. Go to the front of your student, facing them, and **open their hands** out flat. Place your left hand underneath.

2. Draw the **Power symbol over each of their palms**, tapping it in three times while saying the mantra. Visualize the symbol moving into each hand. Then using the open palm of your right hand, lightly pat three times into each of the student's open palms.

3. Return your student's hands to prayer position in front of their heart. In one strong breath (if you can), blow from your student's hands down toward the Base Chakra, then up to the Third Eye, back down to the Solar Plexus, and then end back at the hands. (If you can keep your Hui Yin point contracted while blowing, that is best. If not, it is ok to release it while you blow and then contract it again.)

From back

1. Return to the back of your student, putting your hands on their shoulders. Imagine looking down through the student's crown and into their Heart Chakra. See each of the Reiki symbols inside the chakra. Choose a positive affirmation, such as, **"You are now a powerful and aware Reiki Level I healer."** You are going to place the positive affirmation into their heart. Silently say the affirmation three times with the intention that your student's subconscious accepts it.

2. Visualize a triangular door made by placing your thumbs and fingers at the back of your student's head. Your thumbs (the base of the triangle) should be at or near the occipital ridge. See all the symbols going inside their head, one by one, and then visualize this door being closed and sealed with the Power symbol on the outside. Silently say to your guides, **"I seal this attunement with love and Divine energy."** (Or use something similar that resonates with you.) Intend that the process is complete and that your student's direct connection to the Reiki Source and their Reiki guides is now in place.

3. Once again put your hands on your student's shoulders. Silently say to your guides, **"In this attunement we are both blessed."**

From the front

1. Return to the front, facing your student. Place their hands on their lap, palms facing down. In the case of group attunements, this step is left until all your students have been attuned.

STAGE 2

From behind

1. Standing behind your student, draw the **Fire Serpent symbol** starting at the back of your student's head going down to their Base Chakra.

2. Connect energetically by placing your hands over the top of their head, tuning in.

3. Contract and hold the Hui Yin point, keeping your tongue against the alveolar ridge (throughout the entire attunement). Take three Blue Kidney Breaths to create the Raku energy and then create the **Violet Breath**. Visualize the **Tibetan Master symbol** within the violet light and blow it into the student's head. Visualize the symbol moving from your head, through your breath, into your student's Crown Chakra, and going into the base of their brain. As you visualize this, silently say the mantra of the symbol three times and tap, once each, at the Crown Chakra, the back of the Third Eye, and at the base of the brain.

4. Draw the **Usui Master symbol over your student's head**. Visualize the symbol moving into the Crown Chakra, through the head, to the base of the brain. As you visualize this, silently say the mantra of the symbol three times and tap, once each, at the Crown Chakra, the back of the Third Eye, and at the base of the brain.

5. Repeat step [4], drawing the **Mental/Emotional symbol over the head.**

6. Squeeze your student's left shoulder to let them know to raise their hands above their head. If they do not remember to do so, then gently pull up their hands.

7. While **holding your student's hands, draw the Power symbol** in the air above them. Visualize the symbol going into the hands, through the Crown Chakra, to the base of the brain. As you visualize this, silently say the mantra of the symbol three times and tap, once each, at the fingertips over the Crown Chakra, the back of the Third Eye, and at the base of the brain.

8. Return your student's hands back down to prayer position over the heart.

From the front

1. Go to the front of your student, facing them, and **open their hands** out flat. Place your left hand underneath.

2. Draw the **Power symbol over each of their palms**, tapping it in three times while saying the mantra. Visualize the symbol moving into each hand. Then using the open palm of your right hand, lightly pat three times into each of the student's open palms.

3. Return your student's hands to prayer position in front of their heart. In one strong breath (if you can), blow from your student's hands down toward the Base Chakra, then up to the Third Eye, back down to the Solar Plexus, and then end back at the hands.

From behind

1. Return to the back of your student, putting your hands on their shoulders. Imagine looking down through the student's crown and into their Heart Chakra. See each of the Reiki symbols inside the chakra. Choose a positive affirmation, such as, **"You are now a powerful and aware Reiki Level I healer."** You are going to place the positive affirmation into their heart. Silently say the affirmation three times with the intention that your student's subconscious accepts it.

2. Visualize a triangular door made by placing your thumbs and fingers at the back of your student's head. Your thumbs (the base of the triangle) should be at or near the occipital ridge. See all the symbols going inside their head, one by one, and then visualize this door being closed and

sealed with the Power symbol on the outside. Silently say to your guides, **"I seal this attunement with love and Divine energy."** (Or use something similar that resonates with you.) Intend that the process is complete and that your student's direct connection to the Reiki Source and their Reiki guides is now in place.

3. Once again put your hands on your student's shoulders. Silently say to your guides, **"In this attunement we are both blessed."**

From the front

1. Return to the front, facing your student. Place their hands on their lap, palms facing down. In the case of group attunements, this step is left until all your students have been attuned.

STAGE 3

From behind

1. Standing behind your student, draw the **Fire Serpent symbol** starting at the back of your student's head going down to their Base Chakra.

2. Connect energetically by placing your hands over the top of their head, tuning in.

3. Contract and hold the Hui Yin point, keeping your tongue against the alveolar ridge (throughout the entire attunement). Take three Blue Kidney Breaths to create the Raku energy and then create the **Violet Breath**. Visualize the **Tibetan Master symbol** within the violet light and blow it into the student's head. Visualize the symbol moving from your head, through your breath, into your student's Crown Chakra, and going into the base of their brain. As you visualize this, silently say the mantra of the symbol three times and tap, once each, at the Crown Chakra, the back of the Third Eye, and at the base of the brain.

4. Draw the **Usui Master symbol over your student's head**. Visualize the symbol moving into the Crown Chakra, through the head, to the base of the brain. As you visualize this, silently say the mantra of the symbol three times

and tap, once each, at the Crown Chakra, the back of the Third Eye, and at the base of the brain.

5. Repeat step [4], drawing the **Mental/Emotional symbol over the head.**

6. Squeeze your student's left shoulder to let them know to raise their hands above their head. If they do not remember to do so, then gently pull up their hands.

7. While **holding your student's hands, draw the Power symbol** in the air above them. Visualize the symbol going into the hands, through the Crown Chakra, to the base of the brain. As you visualize this, silently say the mantra of the symbol three times and tap, once each, at the fingertips over the Crown Chakra, the back of the Third Eye, and at the base of the brain.

8. Return your student's hands back down to prayer position over the heart.

From the front

1. Go to the front of your student, facing them, and **open their hands** out flat. Place your left hand underneath.

2. Draw the **Power symbol over each of their palms**, tapping it in three times while silently saying the mantra. Visualize the symbol moving into each hand. Then using the open palm of your right hand, lightly pat three times into each of the student's open palms.

3. Return your student's hands to prayer position in front of their heart. In one strong breath (if you can), blow from your student's hands down toward the Base Chakra, then up to the Third Eye, back down to the Solar Plexus, and then end back at the hands.

From behind

1. Return to the back of your student, putting your hands on their shoulders. Imagine looking down through the student's crown and into their Heart Chakra. See each of the Reiki symbols inside the chakra. Choose a positive affirmation, such as, **"You are now a powerful and aware Reiki Level I healer."**

You are going to place the positive affirmation into their heart. Silently say the affirmation three times with the intention that your student's subconscious accepts it.

2. Visualize a triangular door made by placing your thumbs and fingers at the back of your student's head. Your thumbs (the base of the triangle) should be at or near the occipital ridge. See all the symbols going inside their head, one by one, and then visualize this door being closed and sealed with the Power symbol on the outside. Silently say to your guides, **"I seal this attunement with love and Divine energy."** (Or use something similar that resonates with you.) Intend that the process is complete and that your student's direct connection to the Reiki Source and their Reiki guides is now in place.

3. Once again put your hands on your student's shoulders. Silently say to your guides, **"In this attunement we are both blessed."**

From the front

1. Return to the front, facing your student. Place their hands on their lap, palms facing down. In the case of group attunements, this step is left until all your students have been attuned.

STAGE 4

From behind

1. Standing behind your student, draw the **Fire Serpent symbol** starting at the back of your student's head going down to their Base Chakra.

2. Connect energetically by placing your hands over the top of their head, tuning in.

3. Contract and hold the Hui Yin point, keeping your tongue against the alveolar ridge (throughout the entire attunement). Take three Blue Kidney Breaths to create the Raku energy and then create the **Violet Breath**. Visualize the **Tibetan Master symbol** within the violet light and blow it into

the student's head. Visualize the symbol moving from your head, through your breath, into your student's Crown Chakra, and going into the base of their brain. As you visualize this, silently say the mantra of the symbol three times and tap, once each, at the Crown Chakra, the back of the Third Eye, and at the base of the brain.

4. Draw the **Usui Master symbol over your student's head**. Visualize the symbol moving into the Crown Chakra, through the head, to the base of the brain. As you visualize this, silently say the mantra of the symbol three times and tap, once each, at the Crown Chakra, the back of the Third Eye, and at the base of the brain.

5. Repeat step [4], drawing the **Mental/Emotional symbol over the head.**

6. Repeat step [4], drawing the **Distance symbol over the head.**

7. Squeeze your student's left shoulder to let them know to raise their hands above their head. If they do not remember to do so, then gently pull up their hands.

8. While **holding your student's hands, draw the Power symbol** in the air above them. Visualize the symbol going into the hands, through the Crown Chakra, to the base of the brain. As you visualize this, silently say the mantra of the symbol three times and tap, once each, at the fingertips over the Crown Chakra, the back of the Third Eye, and at the base of the brain.

9. Return your student's hands back down to prayer position over the heart.

From the front

1. Go to the front of your student, facing them, and **open their hands** out flat. Place your left hand underneath.

2. Draw the **Power symbol over each of their palms**, tapping it in three times while silently saying the mantra. Visualize the symbol moving into each hand. Then using the open palm of your right hand, lightly pat three times into each of the student's open palms.

3. Return your student's hands to prayer position in front of their heart. In one strong breath (if you can), blow from your student's hands down toward the Base Chakra, then up to the Third Eye, back down to the Solar Plexus, and then end back at the hands.

From behind

1. Return to the back of your student, putting your hands on their shoulders. Imagine looking down through the student's crown and into their Heart Chakra. See each of the Reiki symbols inside the chakra. Choose a positive affirmation, such as, **"You are now a powerful and aware Reiki Level I healer."** You are going to place the positive affirmation into their heart. Silently say the affirmation three times with the intention that your student's subconscious accepts it.

2. Visualize a triangular door made by placing your thumbs and fingers at the back of your student's head. Your thumbs (the base of the triangle) should be at or near the occipital ridge. See all the symbols going inside their head, one by one, and then visualize this door being closed and sealed with the Power symbol on the outside. Silently say to your guides, **"I seal this attunement with love and Divine energy."** (Or use something similar that resonates with you.) Intend that the process is complete and that your student's direct connection to the Reiki Source and their Reiki guides is now in place.

3. Once again put your hands on your student's shoulders. Silently say to your guides, **"In this attunement we are both blessed."**

From the front

1. Return to the front, facing your student. Place their hands on their lap, palms facing down. In the case of group attunements, this step is left until all your students have been attuned.

2. State a blessing aloud to let your student know the process is complete.

"You are now a powerful and aware
Tibetan Reiki Level I healer."

SECOND DEGREE ATTUNEMENT – TIBETAN

At Level II the attunement given after the symbols have been taught and it is by this process that they are made a part of your student. Through the symbols, the attunement accesses the etheric body more directly as well as empowering the symbols for your student. The Violet Breath is used and the Hui Yin point is held throughout the attunement.

These are the symbols that you will be passing:

Back – Fire Serpent

Crown – Tibetan Master, Usui Master

Hands Above Crown – Power, Mental/Emotional, Distance

Open Palms – Power, Mental/Emotional, Distance

From behind

1. Standing behind your student, draw the **Fire Serpent symbol** starting at the back of your student's head going down to their Base Chakra.

2. Connect energetically by placing your hands over the top of their head, tuning in.

3. Contract and hold the Hui Yin point, keeping your tongue against the alveolar ridge (throughout the entire attunement). Take three Blue Kidney Breaths to create the Raku energy and then create the **Violet Breath**. Visualize the **Tibetan Master symbol** within the violet light and blow it into the student's head. Visualize the symbol moving from your head, through your breath, into your student's Crown Chakra, and going into the base of their brain. As you visualize this, silently say the mantra of the symbol three times and tap, once each, at the Crown Chakra, the back of the Third Eye, and at the base of the brain.

4. Draw the **Usui Master symbol over your student's head**. Visualize the symbol moving into the Crown Chakra, through the head, to the base of the brain. As you visualize this, silently say the mantra of the symbol three times

and tap, once each, at the Crown Chakra, the back of the Third Eye, and at the base of the brain.

5. Squeeze your student's left shoulder to let them know to raise their hands above their head. If they do not remember to do so, then gently pull up their hands.

6. While **holding your student's hands, draw the Power symbol** in the air above them. Visualize the symbol going into the hands, through the Crown Chakra, to the base of the brain. As you visualize this, silently say the mantra of the symbol three times and tap, once each, at the fingertips over the Crown Chakra, the back of the Third Eye, and at the base of the brain.

7. Repeat step [6], drawing the **Mental/Emotional symbol above the hands.**

8. Repeat step [6], drawing the **Distance symbol above the hands.**

9. Return your student's hands back down to prayer position over the heart.

From the front

1. Go to the front of your student, facing them, and **open their hands** out flat. Place your left hand underneath.

2. Draw the **Power symbol over each of their palms**, tapping it in three times while silently saying the mantra. Visualize the symbol moving into each hand. Then using the open palm of your right hand, lightly pat three times into each of the student's open palms.

3. Repeat step [2], drawing the **Mental/Emotional symbol over each palm.**

4. Repeat step [2], drawing the **Distance symbol over each palm.**

5. Return your student's hands to prayer position in front of their heart. In one strong breath (if you can), blow from your student's hands down toward the Base Chakra, then up to the Third Eye, back down to the Solar Plexus, and then end back at the hands. (If you can keep your Hui Yin point contracted while blowing, that is best. If not, it is ok to release it while you blow and then contract it again.)

From behind

1. Return to the back of your student, putting your hands on their shoulders. Imagine looking down through the student's crown and into their Heart Chakra. See each of the Reiki symbols inside the chakra. Choose a positive affirmation, such as, **"You are now a powerful and aware Reiki Level II practitioner."** You are going to place the positive affirmation into their heart. Silently say the affirmation three times with the intention that your student's subconscious accepts it.

2. Visualize a triangular door made by placing your thumbs and fingers at the back of your student's head. Your thumbs (the base of the triangle) should be at or near the occipital ridge. See all the symbols going inside their head, one by one, and then visualize this door being closed and sealed with the Power symbol on the outside. Silently say to your guides, **"I seal this attunement with love and Divine energy."** (Or use something similar that resonates with you.) Intend that the process is complete and that your student's direct connection to the Reiki Source and their Reiki guides is now in place.

3. Once again put your hands on your student's shoulders. Silently say to your guides, **"In this attunement we are both blessed."**

From the front

1. Return to the front, facing your student. Place their hands on their lap, palms facing down. In the case of group attunements, this step is left until all your students have been attuned.

2. State a blessing aloud to let your student know the process is complete.

"You are now a powerful and aware
Tibetan Reiki Level II practitioner."

MASTER ATTUNEMENT – TIBETAN

There is only one attunement for the Master level. There is no Tibetan attunement at ART/Level III in this system. The attunement is given after the symbols have been taught and it is by this process that they are made a part of your student. The Violet Breath is used and the Hui Yin point is held throughout the attunement.

These are the symbols that you will be passing:

Back – Fire Serpent

Crown – Tibetan Master

Hands Above Crown – Tibetan Master, Fire Serpent, Usui Master, Power, Mental/Emotional, Distance

Open Palms – Tibetan Master, Fire Serpent, Usui Master, Power, Mental/Emotional, Distance

From behind

1. Standing behind your student, draw the **Fire Serpent symbol** starting at the back of your student's head going down to their Base Chakra.

2. Connect energetically by placing your hands over the top of their head, tuning in.

3. Contract and hold the Hui Yin point, keeping your tongue against the alveolar ridge (throughout the entire attunement). Take three Blue Kidney Breaths to create the Raku energy and then create the **Violet Breath**. Visualize the **Tibetan Master symbol** within the violet light and blow it into the student's head. Visualize the symbol moving from your head, through your breath, into your student's Crown Chakra, and going into the base of their brain. As you visualize this, silently say the mantra of the symbol three times and tap, once each, at the Crown Chakra, the back of the Third Eye, and at the base of the brain.

4. Squeeze your student's left shoulder to let them know to raise their hands above their head. If they do not remember to do so, then gently pull up their hands.

5. While **holding your student's hands, draw the Tibetan Master symbol** in the air above them. Visualize the symbol going into the hands, through the Crown Chakra, to the base of the brain. As you visualize this, silently say the mantra of the symbol three times and tap, once each, at the fingertips over the Crown Chakra, the back of the Third Eye, and at the base of the brain.

6. Repeat step [5], drawing **Fire Serpent symbol above the hands.**

7. Repeat step [5], drawing **Usui Master symbol above the hands.**

8. Repeat step [5], drawing **Power symbol above the hands.**

9. Repeat step [5], drawing **Mental/Emotional symbol above the hands.**

10. Repeat step [5], drawing the **Distance symbol above the hands.**

11. Return your student's hands back down to prayer position over the heart.

From the front

1. Go to the front of your student, facing them, and **open their hands** out flat. Place your left hand underneath.

2. Draw the **Tibetan Master symbol over each of their palms**, tapping it in three times while silently saying the mantra. Visualize the symbol moving into each hand. Then using the open palm of your right hand, lightly pat three times into each of the student's open palms.

3. Repeat step [2], drawing the **Fire Serpent symbol over each palm.**

4. Repeat step [2], drawing the **Usui Master symbol over each palm.**

5. Repeat step [2], drawing the **Power symbol over each palm.**

6. Repeat step [2], drawing the **Mental/Emotional symbol over each palm.**

7. Repeat step [2], drawing the **Distance symbol over each palm.**

8. Return your student's hands to prayer position in front of their heart. In one strong breath (if you can), blow from your student's hands down toward the Base Chakra, then up to the Third Eye, back down to the Solar

Plexus, and then end back at the hands. (If you can keep your Hui Yin point contracted while blowing, that is best. If not, it is ok to release it while you blow and then contract it again.)

From behind

1. Return to the back of your student, putting your hands on their shoulders. Imagine looking down through the student's crown and into their Heart Chakra. See each of the Reiki symbols inside the chakra. Choose a positive affirmation, such as, **"You are now a powerful and aware Tibetan Reiki Master."** You are going to place the positive affirmation into their heart. Silently say the affirmation three times with the intention that your student's subconscious accepts it.

2. Visualize a triangular door made by placing your thumbs and fingers at the back of your student's head. Your thumbs (the base of the triangle) should be at or near the occipital ridge. See all the symbols going inside their head, one by one, and then visualize this door being closed and sealed with the Power symbol on the outside. Silently say to your guides, **"I seal this attunement with love and Divine energy."** (Or use something similar that resonates with you.) Intend that the process is complete and that your student's direct connection to the Reiki Source and their Reiki guides is now in place.

3. Once again put your hands on your student's shoulders. Silently say to your guides, **"In this attunement we are both blessed."**

From the front

1. Return to the front, facing your student. Place their hands on their lap, palms facing down. In the case of group attunements, this step is left until all your students have been attuned.

2. State a blessing aloud to let your student know the process is complete.

"You are now a powerful and aware Tibetan Reiki Master."

CHAPTER 14

REIKI HEALING ATTUNEMENT

The Reiki healing attunement is given by a Reiki Master to a client for clearing and healing purposes only. It does not initiate the client into Reiki because the symbols are not placed into the client's hands.

In this attunement you are asking your Reiki guides and Masters in spirit to bring a concentrated healing energy to a specific issue or area of the body. This is often more powerful and effective than a regular Reiki treatment. A healing attunement also allows the client's own guides to connect and work with them as well, so you are activating their guides to continue working with them after the session.

> A healing attunement can be more powerful and effective than a regular Reiki treatment.

A healing attunement can be done right before a psychic surgery or cord removal to help your client to be more open to releasing negative energies and attachments. You may then want to do a regular Reiki session afterward. A healing attunement can also be performed at a distance. To do this you will use an object as a surrogate for the client. (See Chapter 16, Distant Attunements.) A person will often feel the effect just as strongly when the healing attunement is performed remotely.

You can perform healing attunements in a small group in a similar way to doing group initiatory (level) attunements. However, I think healing attunements are most effective when done in a one-on-one situation.

Focus on the Block or the Issue

Physical and mental/emotional ailments originate first in our outer bodies. We may attract negative energy, cords, or attachments in our spiritual body from past lives, karma, or situations in this life. They may then manifest into our lives in the form of a negative relationship or situation. We may also become mentally and emotionally involved in these issues, creating negative energy around us that clouds and blocks our chakras which may manifest into a physical condition.

A healing attunement can remove negative thoughts, fears, or feelings that are holding a person back from living their life purpose.

A healing attunement is effective in clearing these negative energies, dissolving these cords and blocks, and removing attachments so that it heals not only the physical body but gives a complete healing at the soul level. It helps a client heal from a physical condition, a condition that is in their mental or emotional auras, and removes negative blocks that may be preventing them from living life to the fullest.

Before the session discuss with your client what issue or ailment that they would like to release. If it is a physical condition, they will be concentrating on the physical ailment itself. They may or may not be aware of emotional or spiritual issues that are connected to this ailment. Explain to the client that there may be an underlying spiritual issue that is causing this ailment and they will need to be willing to address and release the issues that may come up in order to remove the physical ailment. If it is an emotional issue, mental issue, or some kind of block that your client is experiencing, they will also be concentrating on the root cause of those issues and will have to be willing to release this in order to heal.

Explain to your client that they may have to make adjustments in their way of thinking, emotional attachments, or lifestyle in order to receive a complete healing, otherwise the healing may only be temporary as it will re-manifest if it is not released at a soul level.

During the session your client is going to be concentrating on the issue, ailment, or block and working on releasing and allowing the healing.

Living Their Life Purpose

A healing attunement can be used to help your clients achieve their goals and start living a prosperous and fulfilling life following their soul purpose. The reason that a client is having difficulty achieving something or their life does not feel fulfilling is usually because they have attracted negative energies or blocks that are preventing them from experiencing this.

We are born with a life purpose that we may live life in happiness and joy with prosperity and abundance. If there is an area of their life that a client is not happy with, it is not a matter of helping them achieve that, but rather removing the blocks and negative energy that are clouding their natural way of being. A healing attunement can remove negative thoughts, fears, or feelings that are holding them back from living their life purpose.

Sometimes what the client thinks they want is not on their path and is not in their highest good. A healing attunement can help them to realize what their true path is and to ask for the guidance and be open to what will really help them. You (or the client directly) may be given a message about how they should proceed to help them on their path.

PASSING THE HEALING ATTUNEMENT

The client may lie on a massage table as they would for a regular treatment, or they may be seated with their feet on the floor. Their hands should be relaxed at their side or on their lap (but not in the prayer position as you would for other attunements). The following description is for a seated client. You may adapt the positions if the client is lying down.

Call in your Reiki energy and then connect energetically by placing your hands over the top of their head, tuning in. Instruct your client to close their eyes and relax. You may talk them through a short relaxation meditation or put on some soothing music and give them a moment to get into a quiet space. Your client is going to be focusing on their issue or ailment for the purpose of healing it.

You are going to start the session in a similar way to psychic surgery, asking your client to identify the area and concentrate on it.

1. Ask the client to think about the issue they would like to have healed. They can choose to tell you what the issue is or they can keep it private. The healing attunement is just as effective regardless of if you know the issue or not. What is most important is that the client is comfortable.

2. Ask the client to close their eyes, relax, and meditate on the issue. Tell them to keep their eyes closed during the entire process.

3. Ask your client the location of the block or issue. If they don't know, ask them just to "make something up" or "guess." Whatever pops into their head is fine. There are no wrong answers. Locating the issue and giving it an identity will help you to dissolve and remove it.

4. Ask them the following questions to give a tangible appearance to the issue. Having a visual image for you both to focus on facilitates the removal of the problem.
    *   If this issue had a shape, what would it be?
    *   If this issue had a color, what would it be?
    *   If this issue had a texture, what would it be?
    *   If this issue had a smell, what would it be?

Remember, there are no wrong answers and the client doesn't need to answer every question. For example, the issue may not have a "smell."

5. Ask the client if they are ready and willing to release this issue. If they are hesitant, ask them if there is an aspect of the situation that they are ready to forgive and release. For example, they may not be ready to forgive the

person involved, but may be able to understand that there was a reason for the lesson and release the situation. Try to obtain a positive response before continuing with the healing attunement.

6. Ask your client to continue concentrating on releasing this issue that now has an identity, while you continue with the healing attunement.

HEALING ATTUNEMENT

The symbols that you will be passing:

Back – Fire Serpent

Crown (from behind) – Tap the following into the Crown, Third Eye, and Heart – Tibetan Master, Usui Master, Distance, Mental/Emotional, Power

Crown (from the front) – Tap the following into the Third Eye, Heart, and Solar Plexus – Tibetan Master, Usui Master, Distance, Mental/Emotional, Power

Note – In an initiatory attunement the symbols settle at the base of the brain. In a healing attunement they settle in the heart.

From behind

1. Standing behind your client, draw the **Fire Serpent symbol** starting at the back of your client's head going down to their Base Chakra.

2. Contract and hold the Hui Yin point, keeping your tongue against the alveolar ridge (throughout the entire attunement). Take three Blue Kidney Breaths to create the Raku energy and then create the **Violet Breath**. Visualize the **Tibetan Master symbol** within the violet light and blow it into the student's head. Visualize the symbol moving from your head, through your breath, into your student's Crown Chakra, and going into their Heart Chakra. As you visualize this, silently say the mantra of the symbol three times and tap, once each, at the Crown Chakra, the back of the Third Eye, and at the back of the heart.

3. Draw the **Usui Master symbol over your client's head**. Visualize the symbol moving into the Crown Chakra, through the head, to the heart. As you visualize this, silently say the mantra of the symbol three times and tap, once each, at the Crown Chakra, the back of the Third Eye, and at the back of the Heart Chakra.

4. Repeat step [3] drawing the **Power symbol over the Crown Chakra.**

5. Repeat step [3] drawing the **Mental/Emotional symbol over the Crown. Chakra.**

6. Repeat step [3] drawing the **Distance symbol over the Crown Chakra.**

From the front

1. Come back to face the front of your client.

2. Draw the **Tibetan Master symbol over the Crown Chakra**. Tap the crown three times as you silently say the mantra three times. Visualize the symbol moving through the Third Eye, the Heart Chakra, and then into the Solar Plexus.

3. Repeat step [2] drawing the **Usui Master symbol.**

4. Repeat step [2] using the **Power symbol.**

5. Repeat step [2] using the **Mental/Emotional symbol.**

6. Repeat step [2] using the **Distance symbol.**

7. Use your breath to remove the blockage. In one smooth, strong breath, blow starting at the Solar Plexus, up to the heart, the Third Eye, and the crown, then back down to the Solar Plexus, and back up again to the crown, blowing up and out. This is all done in one breath. Utilize your hands, along with the breath, to guide the energy out and up to the light. If the blockage has been assigned a shape by the client, you can visualize this shape as well, exiting to the light. Try to keep your Hui Yin point contracted until the end. If you find this to be difficult, you can release it with your breath. Just contract it again after blowing and then continue with the rest of the attunement.

From behind

1. With your hands on your client's shoulders, look down through their crown and into their Heart Chakra. See their Heart Chakra shining brightly. (The Heart Chakra is an emerald green color, although sometimes other colors such as pink or gold can be seen). State an affirmation silently, such as *"Your heart is filled with Divine love and wisdom"* or what you feel to be appropriate for your client. Say this three times with the intention that it is accepted by your client's subconscious.

2. With your right hand over the back of their Heart Chakra and your left hand on their shoulder, ask your guides to complete and seal this healing attunement. Say, *"I seal this healing with love and Divine energy"* three times silently. (Or use something similar that resonates with you.) Over the Heart Chakra envision a door with the Power symbol on it being closed and locked.

3. Put your hands on your client's shoulders acknowledging that you were both blessed in this process.

From the front

1. Return to the front of your client. With your hands stretched outward, palms facing your client, direct Reiki energy and ask that your client be blessed and healed.

2. With your palm still facing your client's heart, take a breath, hold it, and then release your Hui Yin point as you exhale. As you release, you are offering a blessing to your client.

3. Ask the client to breathe deeply, slowly. Let them know that when they are ready, they may slowly open their eyes.

Continue the Session

Now ask your client if the issue feels resolved or if they feel there is still some residual left. If necessary, you may continue with a psychic surgery and a hands-on session.

CHAPTER 15
PSYCHIC ATTUNEMENTS

You can perform a psychic attunement to open up a person's psychic senses and enhance their psychic abilities. This does not initiate someone into Reiki as no symbols are placed into the hands. You can also perform a psychic attunement on yourself by following the guidelines outlined in the self-attunement section.

CLAIRVOYANT ATTUNEMENT

The clairvoyant sense is associated with the Third Eye therefore most of this attunement's symbols will be placed into the Third Eye Chakra. Additional chakras related to clairvoyance are the Heart Chakra (4th chakra) and the Sacral Chakra (2nd chakra). The Power symbol will be placed into these chakras as well.

The symbols that you will be passing:

Back – Fire Serpent

Channel Reiki to the Third Eye

Crown – Mental/Emotional

Back of the Third Eye – Tibetan Master, Usui Master, Distance, Mental/Emotional

Back of the Heart – Power

Back of the Sacral Chakra – Power

Channel Reiki to the Third Eye

Front of the Third Eye – Power

Front of the Heart – Power

Front of the Sacral Chakra – Power

Channel Reiki to the Third Eye

Back – Raku

From behind

1. Standing behind your client, draw the **Fire Serpent symbol** starting at the back of their head going down to their Base Chakra.

2. Direct **Reiki to the Third Eye** by placing one hand in front of the forehead and one hand at the back of the head. Have the intention that the Reiki is opening and clearing this chakra.

3. Draw the **Mental/Emotional symbol over your client's head**. Visualize the symbol moving into the Crown Chakra, through the head, to the base of the brain. As you visualize this, silently say the mantra of the symbol three times and tap, once each, at the Crown Chakra, the back of the Third Eye, and at the base of the brain.

4. Contract and hold your Hui Yin point. Take three Blue Kidney Breaths to create the Raku energy and then create the **Violet Breath**. Visualize the **Tibetan Master symbol** within the violet light and blow it into the client's head. Visualize the symbol moving from your head into theirs, and to the back of the **Third Eye**. Tap it into the back of the Third Eye Chakra three times silently saying the mantra.

5. Draw the **Usui Master symbol over the back of the Third Eye Chakra**. Tap it in three times along with the mantra.

6. Repeat step [5] with the **Distance symbol.**

7. Repeat step [5] with the **Mental/Emotional symbol.**

8. Draw the **Power symbol over the back of the Heart Chakra**. Tap three times at the back of the Heart Chakra as you silently say the mantra three times.

9. Draw the **Power symbol over the back of the Sacral Chakra** (lower back). Tap three times at the back of the Sacral Chakra as you silently say the mantra three times.

10. Direct **Reiki to the Third Eye** by placing one hand in front of the forehead and one hand at the back of the head. Have the intention that the Reiki is opening and clearing the chakra.

From the front

1. Come to the front of your client, facing them.

2. Draw the **Power symbol over the Third Eye Chakra**. Tap three times as you silently say the mantra of the symbol three times.

3. Draw the **Power symbol over the Heart Chakra**. Tap three times as you silently say the mantra three times.

4. Draw the **Power symbol over the Sacral Chakra**. Tap three times as you silently say the mantra three times.

From behind

1. Direct **Reiki to the Third Eye** by placing one hand in front of the forehead and one hand at the back of the head. Give the intention that the Reiki is opening and clearing the chakra.

2. Draw the **Raku** symbol down the back of your client to seal in the attunement and disconnect your aura from your client's aura. You may release the Hui Yin point as you draw the Raku.

From the front

1. Return to the front of your client and state a blessing aloud to let them know that the process is complete.

"Your clairvoyant sense is now clear and awake."

CLAIRAUDIENT ATTUNEMENT

The clairaudient sense is hearing psychically. It is associated with the Throat Chakra. Therefore, most of the symbols will be placed into the Throat Chakra (4th chakra). Additional Chakras related to clairaudience are the Third Eye Chakra (6th chakra) and the Base Chakra (1st chakra). The power symbol will be placed into these chakras as well.

The symbols that you will be passing:

Back – Fire Serpent

Channel Reiki to the Third Eye

Crown – Mental/Emotional

Back of the Throat Chakra – Tibetan Master, Usui Master, Distance, Mental/Emotional

Back of the Base Chakra – Power

Back of the Third Eye – Power

Channel Reiki to the Throat Chakra

Front of the Throat Chakra – Power

Front of the Base Chakra – Power

Front of the Third Eye – Power

Channel Reiki to the Throat Chakra

Back – Raku

From behind

1. Standing behind your client, draw the **Fire Serpent symbol** starting at the back of their head going down to their Base Chakra.

2. Direct **Reiki to the Third Eye** by placing one hand in front of the forehead and one hand at the back of the head. Have the intention that the Reiki is opening and clearing this chakra.

3. Draw the **Mental/Emotional symbol over your client's head**. Visualize the symbol

moving into the Crown Chakra, through the head, to the base of the brain. As you visualize this, silently say the mantra of the symbol three times and tap, once each, at the Crown Chakra, the back of the Third Eye, and at the base of the brain.

4. Contract and hold your Hui Yin point. Then take three Blue Kidney Breaths to create the Raku energy and then create the **Violet Breath**. Visualize the **Tibetan Master symbol** within the violet light and blow it into the client's head. Visualize the symbol moving from your head into theirs, and to the **Throat Chakra**. Tap it into the back of the Throat Chakra three times silently saying the mantra.

5. Draw the **Usui Master symbol over the Throat Chakra** at the back of the neck. Tap it in three times as you silently say the mantra three times.

6. Repeat step [5] with the **Distance symbol**.

7. Repeat step [5] with the **Mental/Emotional symbol**.

8. Draw the **Power symbol over the Base Chakra** at the base of their spine. Tap three times as you silently say the mantra three times.

9. Draw the **Power symbol over the Third Eye Chakra** at the back of their head. Tap three times as you silently say the mantra three times.

10. Direct **Reiki to the Throat Chakra** by placing one hand in front of the throat and one hand at the back of the neck. Have the intention that the Reiki is opening and clearing this chakra.

From the front

1. Come to the front of your client, facing them.

2. Draw the **Power symbol over the Throat Chakra**. Tap three times as you silently say the mantra three times.

3. Draw the **Power symbol over the Base Chakra**. Tap three times as you silently say the mantra three times.

4. Draw the **Power symbol over the Third Eye Chakra**. Tap three times as you silently say the mantra three times.

From behind

1. Direct **Reiki to the Throat Chakra** by placing one hand in front of the throat and one hand at the back of the neck. Have the intention that the Reiki is opening and clearing this chakra.

2. Draw the **Raku** lightning bolt down the back to signify banking the fire and separating your aura from your client's. You may release the Hui Yin point as you draw the Raku.

From the front

1. Return to the front of your client and state a blessing aloud to let them know that the process is complete.

"Your clairaudient sense is now clear and awake."

CLAIRSENTIENT ATTUNEMENT

The clairsentient sense is feeling psychically. It is associated with the Solar Plexus therefore most of the symbols will be placed into the Solar Plexus Chakra (3rd Chakra). Additional Chakras related to clairsentience are the Heart Chakra (4th chakra) and the Sacral Chakra (2nd chakra). The Power symbol will be placed into these chakras as well.

The symbols that you will be passing:

Back – Fire Serpent

Channel Reiki to the Third Eye

Crown – Mental/Emotional

Back of the Solar Plexus – Tibetan Master, Usui Master, Distance, Mental/Emotional

Back of the Sacral Chakra – Power

Back of the Heart – Power

Channel Reiki to the Solar Plexus

Front of the Solar Plexus – Power

Front of the Sacral Chakra – Power

Front of the Heart– Power

Channel Reiki to the Solar Plexus

Back – Raku

From behind

1. Standing behind your client, draw the **Fire Serpent** symbol starting at the back of the client's head going down to their Base Chakra.

2. Direct **Reiki to the Third Eye** by placing one hand in front of the forehead and one hand at the back of the head. Have the intention that the Reiki is opening and clearing this chakra.

3. Draw the **Mental/Emotional symbol over your client's head**. Visualize the symbol moving into the Crown Chakra, through the head, to the base of the brain. As you visualize this, silently say the mantra of the symbol three times

and tap, once each, at the Crown Chakra, the back of the Third Eye, and at the base of the brain.

4. Contract and hold your Hui Yin point. Then take three Blue Kidney Breaths and create the **Violet Breath**. Visualize the **Tibetan Master symbol** within the violet light and blow it into the client's head. Visualize the symbol moving from your head into theirs, and to the **Solar Plexus Chakra**. Tap it into the Solar Plexus Chakra at the mid-back three times silently saying the mantra.

5. Draw the **Usui Master symbol** over the **Solar Plexus Chakra** at the mid-back. Tap three times as you silently say the mantra three times.

6. Repeat step [5] with the **Distance symbol.**

7. Repeat step [5] with the **Mental/Emotional symbol.**

8. Draw the **Power symbol over the Sacral Chakra** (lower back). Tap three times as you silently say the mantra three times.

9. Draw the **Power symbol over the Heart Chakra**. Tap three times as you silently say the mantra three times.

10. Direct **Reiki to the Solar Plexus** by placing one hand in front of the Solar Plexus and one hand at the lower back. Have the intention that the Reiki is opening and clearing this chakra.

From the front

1. Come to the front of your client, facing them.

2. Draw the **Power symbol over their Solar Plexus Chakra**. Tap three times as you silently say the mantra three times.

3. Draw the **Power symbol over their Sacral Chakra**. Tap three times as you silently say the mantra three times.

4. Draw the **Power symbol over their Heart Chakra**. Tap three times as you silently say the mantra three times.

From behind

1. Direct **Reiki to the Solar Plexus** by placing one hand in front of the Solar Plexus and one hand at the lower back. Have the intention that the Reiki is opening and clearing this chakra.

2. Draw the **Raku** lightning bolt down the back to signify banking the fire and separating your aura from your client's. You may release the Hui Yin point as you draw the Raku.

From the front

1. Return to the front of your client and state a blessing aloud to let them know that the process is complete.

"Your clairsentient sense is now clear and awake."

CHAPTER 16
DISTANT ATTUNEMENTS

Most Reiki Masters agree that it is better to do an initiatory (level) attunement in person from Master to student. Some believe that it can only be done in person. It is my belief that Reiki is meant to be shared with all who truly want the energy and will use it. Some people simply cannot afford the workshop or do not live in an area where Reiki courses are offered. I believe that it is possible to send an attunement to others at a distance and that this is better than no attunement at all. So, in my opinion, it is ok to give attunements at a distance. A student can always repeat the attunement in person later.

Distant Initiatory Attunement

A surrogate can be used in distant attunements. Use a teddy bear, crystal, pillow, or other object placed on a chair to represent the person to whom you intend to send the attunement. You can also write the person's name on a piece of paper and tape it to the front of the chair. Draw the Distance symbol over the surrogate and repeat the recipient's name three times and their location once, intending that the object represent the student and that they will receive the attunement. Proceed with the attunement process on the surrogate object as you would if the person were in the room with you. If you are using a teddy bear, it is easy to envision the bear's head and paws to represent the student's crown and palms. If you are using an object such as a crystal, choose areas on the crystal to represent the crown, the outstretched open palms, and the hands above the crown.

Distant Healing Attunement

A healing attunement can be done at a distance. As described above, connect with your client using the Distance symbol and then use a teddy bear, crystal, or pillow as a surrogate. Proceed with the healing attunement process on the surrogate object as you would if the person was in the room with you. In an in-person healing attunement you would ask your client to visualize an object to be removed. In a distant healing attunement you are using your own intuition to choose and then visualize the object to be removed.

> A distant attunement can be performed for any type of attunement, including initiatory (level) attunements, healing attunements, and psychic attunements.

Beforehand, discuss with your client the issue to be healed. If they wish to keep the specific details private, that is ok, too. Ask them to remain quiet during the time you will be doing the distant healing attunement. If they like, they may visualize the issue being removed. They do not need to know the shape you've chosen (as you are making this choice during the treatment and they aren't physically present); they can simply imagine its removal.

Distant Psychic Attunement

A psychic attunement can be done at a distance. As described above, connect with your client using the Distance symbol and then use a teddy bear, crystal, or pillow as a surrogate. Proceed with the psychic attunement process on the surrogate object as you would if the person was in the room with you.

It is easier to perform a psychic attunement on yourself by doing a distant psychic attunement. For this you would draw the Distance symbol over the surrogate object twice, once to connect at a distance and once to connect into the future when you would be receiving the psychic attunement (such as later that day). A distant psychic attunement is also useful to enhance your own or your client's psychic senses at a specific time, perhaps for an upcoming meeting or important event.

CHAPTER 17

ATTUNING YOURSELF

It is possible to perform a Reiki attunement on yourself. You can also use this technique to perform a Reiki initiatory (level) attunement, healing attunement, or psychic attunement. Since you have already been attuned to the Master level, it is not necessary for you to do the previous level attunements on yourself. However, if you feel you would like a refresher Master attunement, that is perfectly fine. More often you will perform healing or psychic attunements on yourself, rather than the level attunements.

You can use a teddy bear, crystal, pillow, or other object to represent yourself when doing a self-attunement. Do a distant attunement with the object as your surrogate. In this case you will be doing the distant attunement to yourself for the future, even if the future is only in ten minutes time. You will use the Distance symbol twice, once for the distant attunement and once to bring the future into the now.

When performing self-attunemnts, what is important is your intention, along with what you imagine to be true..

Another way to do a self-attunement (not in the future, but in the current time) is to use your legs, bent at the knees. I personally find this to be quite cumbersome and prefer instead to use an object as a surrogate. However, I am presenting it here as an alternative and you can decide for yourself, which you prefer.

Intend that the knee is your head and the thigh is your back. Your left knee and leg represent the backside of your body and the right knee and leg represent the front part of your body.

If you want to do a refresher Reiki initiatory (level) attunement, place your left hand just above your left knee, intending that this one hand represent both hands above your crown. Use your right hand to draw the symbols in the air, picturing them moving down through both hands, and into the knee as if it is your head. You are actually drawing over your left hand but imagining this is both of your hands above your crown.

Then use your opposite, right knee to represent the front of your body. Place your left open hand over your right knee. Intend that your left hand represent both hands open, palms up. Draw the symbols in the air above your left hand and slap both hands together. Then blow over the hands, Third Eye, and Solar Plexus areas, which are represented by the thigh of your right leg.

Return to the left leg, which is representing your back and see the symbols going into your head (represented by your left knee). Create the triangular door on the back of your knee (representing your head) and see the symbols going into the door. Say the affirmations to yourself. Do the Raku over your left thigh, representing your back. Your intention is to seal in the energy. Then move your hand to your right knee, representing coming to the front of yourself, for the completion of the attunement.

Remember, it is your intention that is the most important part of doing attunements, along with what you imagine to be true.

CHAPTER 18
ATTUNEMENT RECIPIENTS

Attunements can be done for practice as well as on animals, children, and those with terminal illnesses.

Practice Attunements

Practice doing attunements on your friends and family. Reiki circles are a great place to practice attunements as well. The initiatory attunements should only be practiced on those who have already received an attunement to the level that you want to practice. While an attunement will last a lifetime and no additional attunements are necessary in order for the person to continue to have Reiki, additional attunements strengthen and refine the Reiki energy that one already has. They can also create spiritual experiences. Healing attunements can be practiced on anyone.

Animal Attunements

Attunements can be done on animals. Many animals are our healing partners. You may find that they snuggle up and want petting when we feel stressed or unwell. What they are actually doing is taking our negative energy away to heal us and then transforming that energy into positive energy.

My animals love to come around me when I give Reiki. One day my dog Akai jumped on my lap. "Do you want some Reiki?" I asked, as this was something she loved to receive. I was surprised by the answer. "I'd like my attunement," she said indignantly. Of course, I had never thought of it. Why not? Since she is my healing dog, it would make sense. So now my dog is attuned to Reiki Level I.

To attune an animal, you can do it directly if they will stay still. Simply draw the symbols over their front paws (you do not need to lift them up). If the animal cannot stay still, you can do a distant attunement. Simply use a surrogate object, like a stuffed animal or a crystal, as described in Chapter 16.

Attunements on Children

Just as you can attune animals, you can attune small children and babies. This would strictly be an attunement for their sake until they are at an age where they could properly learn how to give Reiki to others.

Attunements for People with a Life-limiting Prognosis

People on hospice or with a life-limiting prognosis can benefit greatly from an attunement. The mere act of giving them a Reiki attunement raises their vibrational level and allows them to feel better, thus giving them a sense of control over their body and their life. Once attuned, they can give themselves Reiki treatments to help cope with their journey through life-end.

CHAPTER 19

TEACHING REIKI

PLANNING YOUR REIKI WORKSHOP

Setting Up Your Workshop

Many Reiki Masters are very powerful Reiki channels and good teachers. However, planning and running a workshop requires a skill set that you may not be familiar with. Ask a friend or partner to handle setting up the workshops if you are not comfortable with the organizational/business side of things.

I find that the best way to get started is to just pick a date and announce your Reiki Level I course. A weekend or evening works best for most people. Pick a date at least a month or two in advance to give yourself time to prepare and market your workshop. Give your students a deadline to sign up (say a week or two before). It is also helpful to offer a discount if they sign up early. Having students pre-book will help you to estimate your attendance.

You can start in your own home if it is big enough. If not, see what local hotels, churches, yoga studios, meeting halls, or other venues may have reasonably priced room rentals. Ask a friend to host your workshop in exchange for attending it for free or at a discount.

Start Small

It's ok to start with just two to four students. In fact, any more than five or six would be too large for your first workshop. Plan to have a friend or a helper ready to jump in and partner with a student if you end up with an odd number of people. You want to be free to teach and not have to partner with one of your students during the practice sessions.

Advertising Your Workshop

Starting small using word of mouth to your friends and colleagues may be all you need in the beginning. Post flyers in local spiritual shops, yoga studios, and health food stores. Also look for spiritually oriented websites where you can list your class online.

Have Students Pre-Book

Make sure your students have a way to pay in advance. For example, a PayPal account is easy to set up. Having your students pay a deposit in advance is a good idea since it discourages no-shows. Be sure to collect email addresses. A week before the workshop you should send out an email detailing how your students should prepare and any other pertinent information.

Schedule and Supplies

Plan your day with an approximate schedule. I have included sample schedules from my own workshops. You will need either a Reiki manual for the level you are teaching or, at a minimum, handouts for the main elements of your course. You will also need completion certificates to give out at the end.

You will need something for your students to lie on for their practice sessions. In lieu of massage tables, I use army-style folding cots covered with colorful sheets and pillows. You can also use yoga mats and have your students lie directly on the ground. Any of these options are fine. If there is nice California sunshine, I set up my cots outdoors. You will need one cot/table/mat for each student. I like to arrange them facing me as the instructor. Since the cots I use are low to the ground, I provide pillows for the students to kneel on.

I have a sign-in sheet for the students. Make sure they include their email address so you can follow up with them after the class (in case you don't already have their email). I also like to give everyone a small gift package when they arrive. Usually this is a purple candle, sage, and fresh flowers. This is optional, but I think students enjoy receiving a little gift.

I provide a full meal (usually lunch depending on the time of the workshop). This is not necessary for you to do, but providing at least water and some snacks would be much appreciated. Many people like to fast before their attunement, so I don't serve the meal until after the attunements. I prefer for the refreshments and meal to be healthy foods.

Setting Up Your Area

You will need a large enough space that you can place a cot, yoga mat, or massage table for each student to comfortably work. Have them set up prior to the start of the workshop (unless your students are bringing their own yoga mats). Prepare your teaching space as previously described using sage, the Reiki symbols, etc. I do most of my workshops at my ranch in California so I schedule some time for the class outside in nature.

Do a Practice Run

Before your first workshop it is helpful do a practice run-through with a couple of friends. If you are preparing on your own, at a minimum you'll want to go over each of the parts of your workshop and how you plan to execute them in your space.

Then relax and have fun!

CHAPTER 20

SAMPLE WORKSHOP REIKI LEVEL I

The following is an example of what one of my Reiki Level I workshops might look like. It is a full day, lasting approximately six hours.

Supplies

Reiki Level I manual for each student

Reiki Level I certificate for each student

Reiki candle gift for each student (optional)

River rocks (optional)

Refreshments

Pendulums for the students to use

Massage table/cot/yoga mat – one per student

REIKI LEVEL I SCHEDULE

12:00 p.m.	Introduction, meet and greet
12:15 p.m.	Meet your Reiki guide meditation
12:30 p.m.	Angel blessings
12:45 p.m.	Reiki manual – discussion and excerpts, passing energy
1:30 p.m.	Gratitude walk, collect stones
2:00 p.m.	Attunement preparation

2:15 p.m.	ATTUNEMENTS (Students will be attuned individually)
	Lunch, reflection cards, personal reflection/meditation
3:30 p.m.	Self-healing tutorial, hand positions
4:00 p.m.	Practice sessions (giving and receiving)
5:00 p.m.	How to use a pendulum, clearing chakras
5:30 p.m.	Crystals and other healing modalities
5:45 p.m.	Closing
6:00 p.m.	Certificates

Meet and Greet

Before the workshop, I send out Reiki preparation instructions. These instructions include meditation in preparation for your Reiki journey as well as dietary suggestions to clear your energetic field. There is guidance for those who wish to fast, cleanse, or at least limit their dietary consumption before their attunement. Some people choose to do a three-day fast, some for just a day. Others don't fast at all. It's a personal choice.

When people arrive for the workshop, I try not to tempt the fasting ones and only put out water and decaffeinated teas. When it is time for the attunements, I attune the fasting ones first so that they can begin their lunch first.

I like to begin by having everyone introduce themselves and talk about how they discovered Reiki. I find that my workshops include people from all walks of life. Some have no background in healing and this is their first introduction to spirituality. Others are professional psychics and healers who wish to add Reiki to the services they offer. With each group I find that a common bond develops and these people often stay connected and continue to grow spiritually together.

I provide each student with a manual as well as a small gift. My gift may consist of a purple candle on a non-flammable dish as well as some herbs and sage that grow at my ranch.

My Introduction

I open by telling my students how I got started on my Reiki journey and how it has changed my life. I also discuss the basics of what Reiki is and what to expect today.

Meet Your Reiki Guides

I next lead my students on a guided meditation to meet their Reiki guides. I begin by guiding them through how to protect, which should be done before any spiritual work. We then begin the meditation. Since the Reiki guides already know that their person is coming to the workshop, they are always there, ready for their person to be attuned as well as excited to begin working with them. Students are often surprised that they are able to sense or see details of their guides.

Angel Blessing

I pass out an angel blessing card to each person at the beginning of the day. Often these blessings turn out to have a very pertinent message. At the end of the day we check back on our blessings, and oftentimes these messages have shown to be surprisingly relevant.

The Reiki Manual

I do a short run-through of the manual. I share the history of Reiki, stories of Dr. Usui, the basic principles and ideals of Reiki, and how to use Reiki. The different levels of Reiki are introduced as well as chakras, auras, and other concepts that we are going to be using. We also discuss the beginning of your Reiki journey.

Passing Energy

Even before having had a Reiki attunement, we all sense, to a certain degree, feelings and energies and can pass energy from one to another. To demonstrate this and show that we already have this ability, we do an exercise of passing energy. The students pair up and decide who is going to be the receiver and who is going to be the sender. The sender is then guided that they are going to be sending the feeling of love. They are asked to put this feeling into the form of a shape, giving this shape a color and smell. They are to imagine this shape and its attributes, and then choose an animal to pass it and this love to the receiver. However, they do not tell the receiver any of this information. The receiver is going to try to energetically sense the shape, its attributes, and the animal that is being sent. The receiver is simply to allow the waves of messages and feelings to pass over them and then to share what they receive. The partners then switch, so each person can experience both sending and receiving.

It is always amazing how many people are able to sense many of the aspects of the energy that is being sent. Some of the receivers are able to describe the shape and its attributes nearly completely. I've even seen senders pick a color and then switch it in their mind just as they are sending it, and the recipient picks up on both colors!

Gratitude Walk

This is probably my favorite part of the day. I live on a ranch and am blessed to be able to include nature in my workshops. I teach the workshop outdoors and include a trip to my stream on the gratitude walk.

As we walk to the stream, I ask my students to think about nature and to be grateful for the beautiful nature around us, really noticing and appreciating the flowers, trees and the little animals. I then ask them to think about what they are grateful for in their lives, their family, their work, and their ability to be here today. I instruct everyone that whenever negative thoughts creep in, like "I am grateful for my teenager but I just wish they would listen to me..." that they immediately override it with a positive thought.

I take my students to a very picturesque spot at the stream where the water cascades over a small waterfall. The riverbed is filled with pebbles and stones. I instruct my students to choose 21 stones from the river. These 21 stones represent the 21 stones that Dr. Usui used on his retreat in the mountains to count out his 21 days. Everyone then takes a moment at the riverbed to contemplate their lives and what they are grateful for, while listening to the soothing sounds of the waterfall. I take each student's stones. First I cleanse them under the running waterfall and then charge them with my Reiki energy before giving them back to the student. I bless and send Reiki to Mother Earth as I have taken these stones from her. I also scatter seeds to thank Mother Earth. It is a Native American tradition to give something back when you take a stone, a feather, or some object from the land. This is a tradition that I like and honor.

These are the 21 stones that my students will use to count out the 21 self-healing sessions required for their Level I certification. I instruct them to place a Reiki candle and dish by their bed and to lay the stones on the dish. Then as they do each self-healing session, take one stone away and put it in another container.

When all the stones are gone, the student has finished their 21 self-healing treatments. This is an easy way to keep track of how many healings have been done, especially if the sessions are not always done on consecutive nights.

On the way back from the river the students are asked to be grateful for something they wish to receive in their lives. I tell them to feel grateful as if it were already theirs because it is already on the psychic plane waiting to manifest for them. We also collect different types of sage, rosemary, lavender, and lemon verbena that I am lucky to have growing on the ranch. The sage we will use for smudging and the herbs to give nice atmosphere to our Reiki sessions.

Preparing for the Attunement

I like to explain exactly what is going to happen during the attunement. I tell everyone that each person will be doing a private attunement with me and let them know how they'll be seated and how to place their hands. I also explain what it may feel like and what to expect. Some Reiki Masters like to keep their students in the dark about what is happening. I think students get more out of it if they can understand what is going on.

ATTUNEMENTS

I prefer to attune each student individually in a separate room. I smudge each student, say my blessings, and then perform the attunement. This takes about 8-10 minutes per student. For a class of 6-8 students, it will take about an hour. Some Reiki Masters prefer to attune all their students together and have them sit in quiet meditation until all of the attunements have been given. Whether to attune your own students individually or in a group is your personal preference.

A meal is served during the attunements. I attune the students who have been fasting first. Those who are not fasting can eat before their attunement if they so desire.

My students are also given tasks to do:

1. After their attunement, practice performing Reiki on a plant or to Mother Earth.
2. I put out various Reiki books to look through.

3. Take a "Reflection Card." Students are told to ask their Reiki guides for any insights that they would like to give and he or she picks a card for the answer.

4. Review the hand positions for self-healing, which will be taught next.

Receiving the Attunement

The student is seated in a chair starting with their hands in the prayer position. I instruct the student to concentrate on the energy coming from their Reiki guides and Masters in spirit who are going to be working with them. Then I proceed with the attunement. During the attunement, I will gently squeeze the student's shoulder when I want them to raise their hands above their Crown Chakra. The student keeps their eyes closed during the attunement and my chants are done silently so the student may not be aware of what is happening. Usually the student will feel the energy as a heat or light sensation, or a tingling through their body. They may feel energized and sometimes a little disorientated.

Blessing Mother Earth

While I am attuning a student, the others have assignments to do. Their first Reiki assignment after their attunement is to practice sending Reiki to Mother Earth. They are to go outside and choose a flower, a plant, or just the ground. Then they call in their Reiki guides and Masters and ask the Reiki energy to flow. The student then places their hands just above the plant or the ground and sends Reiki energy.

Reflection Cards

Another assignment is to use Reiki while asking a question using my reflection card deck. The student calls in their Reiki guides and Masters in spirit and asks them a question. The student then chooses a reflection card. The card chosen is their Reiki guide's answer to their question.

Self-Healing

It is important that we learn to heal ourselves first, as this allows us to be a clearer and therefore stronger channel. We learn the self-healing hand positions and I guide my students through a self-healing session. We hold each position for just a few minutes or however long we feel is necessary. I explain to my students that the hand positions do not have to be exact and that what is most important is their intention. We practice doing the self-healing hand positions both sitting and lying down. This is the first of the 21 self-healing sessions that they need to complete.

Practice Sessions

This is the part everyone has been waiting for. We partner up to do practice hands-on Reiki sessions. Each student gets the opportunity to both send and receive. I usually face the Reiki beds so that the students can see me and I guide them through an example of a hands-on session. The recipient simply enjoys the experience. I then have the partners discuss it so that the receiver can share what they felt and the sender can explain what they sensed. Most of the time students are surprised at what they pick up and the receiver often feels strong energy.

Pendulums

We learn how to use pendulums for yes/no questions and for checking the chakras. Now we repeat the practice session, this time incorporating the pendulum to check the chakras.

Crystals

We discuss the energy of crystals and their use in Reiki. We may also do a mini-practice session using crystals.

Other Notes

We discuss the many uses of Reiki and how it can be incorporated into other modalities that the students may be practicing or would like to learn. This is a great time for any other questions and final discussions.

Closing

I issue the certificates on the same day. It is up to the student to do their 21 days of self-healing and then to start using this beautiful energy.

CHAPTER 21

SAMPLE WORKSHOP REIKI LEVEL II

The following is an example of what one of my Reiki Level II workshops might look like. It is a full day, lasting approximately nine hours.

Supplies

Reiki Level II manual for each student

Reiki Level II certificate for each student

Reiki candle gift for each student (optional)

Craft supplies such as pillowcases, markers, plant pots, soil, and seeds (optional)

Refreshments

Pendulums for the students to use

Massage table/cot/yoga mat – one per student

REIKI LEVEL II SCHEDULE

10:30 a.m. Meet and greet. Open the sacred space.

10:45 a.m. Share Reiki experiences. What to expect at Level II. Hand out manuals.

11:00 a.m. Discuss the Level II symbols and incorporate them in art projects.

POWER – Draw the symbol on river rocks and pillowcases

MENTAL/EMOTIONAL – Draw the symbol on pillowcases

DISTANCE – Draw the symbol on pillowcases

12:00 p.m.	Prepare for the attunement. Meditation to meet your Reiki guides.
12:15 p.m.	ATTUNEMENTS (Students will be attuned individually)
	Lunch and Reiki practice
1:15 p.m.	Self-healing using the symbols.
1:30 p.m.	Practice sessions using the symbols. Do a Mental/Emotional treatment.
2:30 p.m.	Break
2:45 p.m.	How to do a sitting session.
3:00 p.m.	Distance healings. Make a Reiki pouch. Animal Reiki. Group healing for the world.
4:00 p.m.	How to do a manifesting session.
4.15 p.m.	Symbols for protection, removing negative energy. Reiki to a future event.
4:30 p.m.	Break
5:00 p.m.	Heal past life/early life issues with the help of a pendulum and your guides.
6:00 p.m.	Practice sessions. Auras, energy fields, seeing spirits, receiving messages.
7:00 p.m.	Questions. Working as Reiki practitioner. Setting up your own business.
7:30 p.m.	Certificates

Meet and Greet

I like to have everyone introduce themselves and then we open the sacred space. I provide each student with a manual and a little gift. My gift may consist of a purple candle on a candle dish and some herbs and sage that grow at my ranch.

Reiki I Experiences and an Introduction to Level II

The students share their experiences so far with Reiki. We review what changes may have occurred in the student since their Level I attunement, how they are incorporating Reiki into their life, and any questions they may have so far. I also give a brief introduction about what they will be learning at Level II.

Learning the Symbols

At Reiki Level II we learn three of the sacred symbols.

THE POWER SYMBOL

THE MENTAL/EMOTIONAL SYMBOL

THE DISTANCE SYMBOL

We discuss the history and meaning of each symbol as well as how to draw and use them in a Reiki session. I also like to add some arts and crafts, which may include:

- River rocks – Choose seven river rocks and draw the Power symbol on each to represent the seven main chakras. Sometimes we may lay the stones out in a line, like the chakras, and do a Reiki session on them.

- Pillowcases – Draw or paint the three symbols on a pillowcase. The students can then use this pillow on their Reiki bed. Although, I suggest using the pillow facedown so that the client can't see the symbols.

- Reiki box – Take an unfinished box and decorate it with the three symbols. This is a great place to store notes of what you would like to manifest. You can also put the names of friends and clients who you wish to receive Reiki inside.

- Plant pot – We take undecorated pots and paint the three symbols on them. We then fill the pots with soil from around my ranch and plant seeds in it. We do Reiki on the plant for it to grow. I like to use herb or vegetable seeds so that you can eat the plants that grow from this beautiful Reiki energy.

Reiki Guides

At Level II we go more in-depth about working with our guides. During our sessions we will concentrate on tuning in and being guided by our Reiki Masters in spirit. I prepare my students for a meditation and guide them through the white light protection. Then I lead a guided meditation for them to become more deeply aware of their Reiki Guides. Usually at Level II a student's awareness of their guides increases.

Attunements, Lunch, and Practicing Using the New Energy

The class breaks for lunch while I give the attunements. I attune the fasting ones first so that they can begin eating more quickly. Students may have lunch, review the symbols, meditate and reflect, and send Reiki to the earth. After they've been attuned, I ask the students to find a partner and practice sending the Reiki energy to each other using the symbols.

Receiving the Attunement

As I explained, I like to do individual attunements. The student sits in a chair starting with their hands in the prayer position. At Level II the student will often feel the energy more dramatically. It may feel like a heat or light sensation or a tingling through their body. They may feel energized and sometimes a little disorientated. It is usually similar to what the student experienced at Level I but stronger.

Self-Healing Using the Symbols

I lead the students in a self-healing session using the symbols that were activated in their palms during the attunement.

Practice Sessions Using the Symbols

The students partner-up for practice hands-on sessions, incorporating the symbols and using a pendulum. They will concentrate on receiving guidance from the spirit world and using their psychic senses.

How to Do a Mental/Emotional Session

I explain how to do a Mental/Emotional treatment. This is often used at the beginning of a session. The students practice it on each other.

How to Do a Sitting Session

I explain the hand positions for performing a sitting session.

Distance Healing

I teach how to do a distance healing to send Reiki to a person that is not present in the room. Using a teddy bear, the students practice how they would send Reiki to a friend or loved one who is not present.

World Healing

The group chooses a world event that needs healing right now and we do a world event Reiki healing session together as a group.

Distance Healing For Manifesting

I teach how to do a distance healing to help you to manifest something. We make a Reiki pouch so that you can manifest all your desires.

Distance Healing to the Future

I teach how to send a distance healing into the future. We practice by sending Reiki to ourselves in the future for an important event coming up.

Protection and Clearing Negative Energy

We learn how to use our Reiki Level II symbols for protection and to clear negative energy.

Distance Healing for Past Life Issues

We learn how to send Reiki to a past life to heal a specific issue. We learn how to use the pendulum to determine the year when this issue first began.

Starting Your Reiki Practice

We discuss setting up your own business as a Reiki practitioner and working professionally.

Certificates

I usually give out the Level II certificates at the end of class and trust that the student will complete the requirements. The commitment to complete the Level II requirements is with each student's Reiki spirit guide, not to me.

CHAPTER 22

SAMPLE WORKSHOP ART/LEVEL III

The following is an example of what one of my Advanced Reiki Training (ART)/Level III workshops might look like. It is two separate days for a total length of ten and a half hours. The course can also be taught in a single day.

Supplies

Reiki Level III/ART manual for each student

Reiki Level III/ART certificate for each student

Reiki candle gift for each student (optional)

Refreshments

Crystals and crystal grid

Pendulums for the students to use

Massage table/cot/yoga mat for each student is optional because all the techniques can be taught using a chair.

SAMPLE WORKSHOP – ART/REIKI LEVEL III

The following schedule is for two separate days, a total length of ten and a half hours. The course can also be taught in a single day.

Day 1	6:00 p.m. – 9:30 p.m.
6:00 p.m.	Meet and greet
6:30 p.m.	Discuss the levels of Reiki, ART and Master
6:45 p.m.	Reiki guides meditation
7:00 p.m.	The Usui Master symbol
7:30 p.m.	Preparing for the Level III attunement
7:45 p.m.	ATTUNEMENTS
	(Refreshments)
8:45 p.m.	Using the Usui Master symbol
9:00 p.m.	Practice sending the Usui Master symbol to each other
9:30 p.m.	Closing

Day 2	11:00 a.m. – 6 p.m.
11:00 a.m.	Check-in. Discuss post-attunement experiences and changes
11:30 a.m.	Choose crystals for the Reiki Crystal Grid
11:45 a.m.	Reiki Moving Meditation
12:15 p.m.	The Antahkarana symbol and other symbols
12:30 p.m.	Crystals and the Reiki Crystal Grid
1:30 p.m.	Lunch
2:30 p.m.	Psychic surgery demonstration
3:00 p.m.	Psychic surgery practice sessions
4:00 p.m.	Break
4:15 p.m.	Cutting negative psychic cords demonstration. Past life healing
4:30 p.m.	Cutting cords practice
5:30 p.m.	Enhancing the Third Eye
6:00 p.m.	Closing and certificates

Meet and Greet

The students share the changes they have already experienced thus far, and we discuss what to expect at Level III.

Discuss the Levels of Reiki, ART and Master

We discuss the differences between ART/Level III and the Masters, the benefits of teaching these separately, and how this program was developed.

Reiki Guides Meditation

I talk more in-depth about our spirit guide connection. I lead a guided meditation to further connect with our guides.

The Usui Master Symbol

I teach the Usui Master symbol, it's meaning and uses. The students also practice drawing the different versions.

Preparing for the Level III Attunement

We discuss what to expect during the Level III attunement and any potential differences from the prior levels.

ATTUNEMENTS

I like to do the attunements individually. Once a student has been attuned, they can have a snack and do practice exercises. These include drawing the Usui Master symbol and practicing using it.

Using the Usui Master Symbol

I teach the students how to incorporate the Usui Master symbol into various Reiki treatments and sessions.

Practice Sending the Usui Master Symbol

The students practice sending the Usui Master symbol to each other, feeling the difference in the energy.

Choose Crystals for the Reiki Crystal Grid

I introduce the Reiki Crystal Grid that we will be making later. Now I have the students choose their crystals, cleanse them, and put them outside in the sun to charge them. This way the crystals will be ready to use when we make the grid later in the day.

Reiki Moving Meditation

This is a nice break to stretch and move. We do a Reiki Moving Meditation together using the Usui Master symbol.

The Antahkarana Symbol and Other Symbols

We discuss the Antahkarana symbol, how it can be used in Reiki, and the students practice drawing it. I introduce the Manifesting symbol, how to use it, and how to draw it. We discuss other symbols, such as the OM symbol.

Crystals and the Reiki Crystal Grid

We discuss working with crystals in a Reiki session. We make a Reiki Crystal Grid using the crystals that we charged in the sun. I instruct the students on how to charge their grid and use it for manifesting and healing.

Psychic Surgery

I demonstrate how to do a psychic surgery. The students then partner up to do a practice session incorporating a psychic surgery. Each student experiences both giving and receiving a psychic surgery.

Cutting Negative Psychic Cords

I demonstrate how to do cutting cords. We discuss how to detect and remove them as well as how to resolve the issues between the people involved. If a past life is involved, we discuss how to send Reiki to the past. The students then partner up to practice cutting cords on each other.

Enhancing the Third Eye

I demonstrate how to give Reiki to the Third Eye, both on another and to oneself. Students then practice opening up each other's Third Eye.

Certificates

My students receive their ART/Level III certificates.

CHAPTER 23

SAMPLE WORKSHOP
REIKI MASTER

The following is an example of what one of my Reiki Master workshops might look like. It is two separate days for a total length of ten hours. The course can also be taught in a single day.

Supplies

Reiki Master manual for each student

Reiki Master certificate for each student

Reiki candle gift for each student (optional)

Refreshments

REIKI MASTER SCHEDULE

DAY 1	11:00 a.m. – 6:00 p.m.
11:00 a.m.	Discuss Reiki Level III experiences. Introduction to the Master level
11:30 a.m.	Reiki Moving Meditation
12:00 p.m.	Discuss key points in the Master manual
12:15 p.m.	The Tibetan Master symbol
12:45 p.m.	ATTUNEMENTS (Students will be attuned individually.) Refreshments/lunch
1:45 p.m.	Other symbols – Raku, Fire Serpent
2:15 p.m.	Breathing techniques – Blue Kidney Breath, Violet Breath

1:00 p.m.	Learning to pass attunements – Level I
1:30 p.m.	Practice passing Level I attunements
2:30 p.m.	Break
2:45 p.m.	Learning to pass attunements – Level II
3:00 p.m.	Practice passing Level II attunements
3:30 p.m.	Learning to pass attunements – Level III
3:45 p.m.	Practice passing Level III attunements
4:00 p.m.	Break
4:15 p.m.	Learning to pass attunements – Master
4:30 p.m.	Practice passing Master attunements
DAY 2	6:30 pm – 9:30 pm
6:30 p.m.	Group sharing
7:00 p.m.	Learning to pass healing attunements
7:30 p.m.	Practice passing healing attunements
8:00 p.m.	Break
8:15 p.m.	Learning to pass psychic attunements
8:30 p.m.	Practice passing psychic attunements
9:00 p.m.	Final questions, running a Reiki business, teaching Reiki, certificates
9:30 p.m.	Closing

Introduction to the Master level

We discuss what the student has learned so far and where they hope to go with their Master training.

Reiki Moving Meditation

I lead a Reiki Moving Meditation to call in our guides and set the tone for the day.

Master Manual

I go through the Master manual and we discuss key points.

Tibetan Master symbol

I teach the Tibetan Master symbol. The students practice drawing it and we discuss how to use it in our Reiki sessions.

ATTUNEMENTS

I prefer to do the attunements individually. The students are instructed to practice drawing the Tibetan Master symbol and once they are attuned, they can practice using it. Lunch is also served.

Symbols – Raku, Tibetan Fire Serpent

We learn the Raku and Tibetan Fire Serpent symbols and their uses.

Breathing Techniques – Blue Kidney Breath, Violet Breath

We learn the breathing techniques and how to pass the Tibetan Master symbol using these techniques.

Learning to Pass Initiatory Attunements

I demonstrate and then teach the initiatory attunements. I like to teach the Blaji version first. I teach each level individually and allow the students to practice on each other before moving on to the next level. After the students are familiar with the four Blaji attunements, I show them the Usui (long version) and Tibetan attunements.

Learning to Pass Healing Attunements

I demonstrate and then teach the healing attunement. The students then partner up and practice on each other.

Learning to Pass Psychic Attunements

I demonstrate and then teach each of the psychic attunements (clairvoyant, clairaudient, clairsentient). The students partner up and practice each attunement on each other.

Teaching Reiki

We discuss the practicalities of teaching Reiki, doing Reiki workshops, and setting up a Reiki school.

Certificates

The students receive their Master certificate.

ONGOING REIKI WORKSHOPS

Periodically I organize Reiki exchange days. These allow the students to practice Reiki with other students. Usually my students at all levels, including Reiki Master, attend. This is a great place to explore and exchange ideas. Some Reiki students use these workshops to do their Level II homework sessions. Others incorporate different modalities into their Reiki and it is a great opportunity for them to feel free to improvise and receive feedback. I may also arrange workshops that concentrate on one or more aspects of Reiki, for example, cutting cords or distance healing. Our Reiki journey is never complete and I find that people always find something new whenever they review or further develop their Reiki.

THE LEVEL II SYMBOLS

Power Symbol
Cho Ku Rey

Mental/Emotional Symbol
Sei Hei Ki

Distance Symbol
Hon Sha Za Sho Nen

APPENDIX B
REIKI LINEAGE

You have now become a certified Reiki Master and are part of a Reiki lineage. Similar to a family tree, your Reiki lineage can be traced back through each Reiki Master to Dr. Usui himself. As a newly indoctrinated Reiki Master, your place in your lineage will be under the Reiki Master that you were attuned by. Some Reiki Masters may study under and receive an attunement from more than one Master. In this case they would be placed more than once on the Reiki family tree.

The students you initiate as Reiki Masters will take their place under you. It is interesting to note which Reiki Masters are in your lineage and if they have added something specific to your Reiki path.

My lineage is on the following page. If you were attuned by me at the Master level, then your name would be placed under mine (and you would be included on more than one branch).

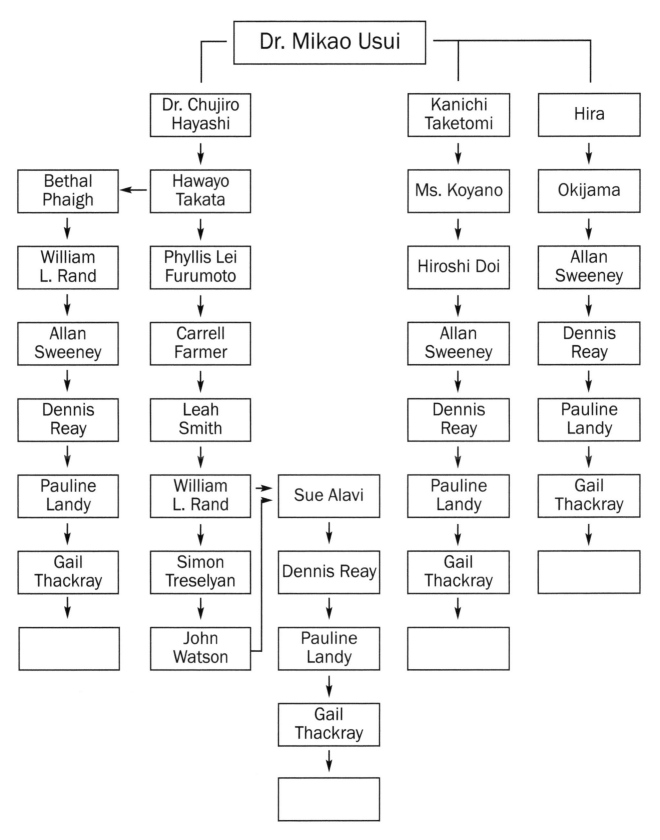

ACKNOWLEDGMENTS

Your Reiki journey is not completing, but rather it has just begun. As you travel down this path, I hope you will research, read, learn, and experience through the many works of those who spread the word of Reiki as well as meet many other Reiki practitioners.

Just as you continue your Reiki search, so do I. It is from this continuous journey that I have collected the many truths contained herein. Some information here has been passed down from my Auntie Pauline and her Reiki Masters. Some has been gathered from my own continuous Reiki search. Some has been Divinely guided. I have endeavored to provide you with all the elements of the traditional Reiki Usui system as well as other material I present here for your consideration on your Reiki path.

My first and very special thanks goes to my auntie:

Reiki Master, **Pauline Landy**

For without Pauline, I may never have been introduced to this wonderful energy and, through this, my connection to Source, which has lit the spiritual path of my life.

And to her son:

Reiki Master, **Ric Landy**

Who continues to support and inspire me on my Reiki journey.

Additionally, I would like to thank the Masters in my Reiki lineage who have contributed to my attunement and to those Masters who spread the word and knowledge through their devotion to teaching and authoring on Reiki. In particular:

Pat Hudson, William Rand, Simon Treselyan, and John Watson

And of course for the lineage of Reiki itself:

Mikao Usui, Chujiro Hayashi, and Hawayo Takata

And all my Reiki Masters and Guides in spirit

With thanks for the support of my family, friends, assistants, and Reiki students who have helped and supported me in my teaching, especially **my mom** and **my daughters**, and my Reiki Master students, **Donna, Vicky, Robert,** and **Cindy**. And to my dear friend, **Mara**, who oversaw the production of my Reiki books and without whom they probably would never have been published.

ABOUT THE AUTHOR

Gail Thackray was raised in Yorkshire, England and prides herself on having kept her English down-to-earth sensibility. Her life changed at age forty when she discovered she was a medium and able to talk to spirits on the other side. Gail attributes her opening to the psychic world to her first Reiki attunement. Helping others connect to Source and to develop their own natural healing and psychic abilities is her passion. Gail lectures at events worldwide, doing live appearances as a healer, medium, and educator. When at home in Los Angeles, she writes, lectures, and teaches about mediumship, Reiki, animal communication, manifesting, and other aspects of spirituality.

Reiki Certification Manuals by Gail Thackray:

Reiki Level I – Energy Healing for Beginners

Reiki Level II – Practitioner Level Energy Healing

Reiki Level III/ART – Advanced Practitioner Level Energy Healing

Reiki Master – Master/Teacher Level Energy Healing

Reiki DVDs by Gail Thackray:

Reiki Level I – Workshop and attunement DVD

Reiki Level II – Workshop and attunement DVD

Reiki Level III/ART – Workshop and attunement DVD

Reiki Master – Workshop and attunement DVD

To order or for information on Gail's books, CDs, and DVDs on Reiki, energy healing, and other spiritual subjects, please go to:

www.GailThackray.com

Milton Keynes UK
Ingram Content Group UK Ltd.
UKHW051346121123
432429UK00017B/372